THE ENEMY AMONG US

THE ENEMY AMONG US

A Story of Witch-hunting in the McCarthy Era

Written & Illustrated by Frank Rowe

Foreword by Carey McWilliams

Cougar Books

Book design by Jon Goodchild
Edited by Suzanne Lipsett

Printed in the U.S.A.   ⑧

Library of Congress #79-56759
ISBN 0-917982-18-5

To our grandchildren

FOREWORD

by Carey McWilliams

FRANK ROWE'S STORY of persecution in the McCarthy
era is an extraordinarily moving and significant
account of a key incident of the period, one that will
not go away and that refuses to be forgotten. It is also
a splendid example of the importance of "personal
history" as an indispensable supplement to the formal or official
variety. There have been studies of the stupid and cruel Levering
Act and the issues it raised. But these studies, despite their merits,
fail to convey a sense of the human, social, and political aspects
of the long struggle to correct, if belatedly and inadequately,
the injustices and hardships enforcement of the act caused.

Frank Rowe tells the story as it should be told, in a quiet,
matter-of-fact manner, without a trace of self-righteousness and
with no breast-beating. And he is just the right person to tell the
story: an artist, without any left-wing ideological hang-ups or
strong political biases. He simply could not abide the thought of
signing a test oath which he profoundly and correctly believed
violated the spirit and the letter of the Constitution and the
First Amendment.

A modest man, he is also candid and direct; he assumes no
postures and indulges in no fancy rhetoric. He tells his personal
story—and a most dramatic and significant story it is—without
flourishes or fancy cadenzas. And because it is told in this manner
it is wholly convincing.

As a people, we have never liked to ponder the meaning
of shabby episodes in our nation's history during which a majority
of Americans have, momentarily at least, forgotten the meaning
of the Bill of Rights, knuckled under to the noisy tirades of
demagogues, and demonstrated a shocking opportunism. Once

these disgraceful episodes have abated, it is most embarrassing for those whose silence or approval made them possible to be reminded of what happened; they avert their eyes from the sordid record and do not like to be told of who did what, where, and when. Invariably a conscious effort is made, usually furthered by the media, to make the episode appear less shameful than in fact it was and, also, to convince a later generation that it could not happen again.

To overcome or at least partially to offset this tendency, we need to be reminded of what happened, however painful the process, and Frank Rowe's fine memoir serves this purpose admirably. He reminds us, for example, of the setting, of the scare headlines, of Korea, of the Hiss and Rosenberg cases, of the inquisitorial hearings, of the purges and blacklists, of the obsession with loyalty. In a most convincing manner, he explains what a cruel choice it was for a person of modest means and family responsibilities to make that fateful decision: to sign or not to sign.

The consequences either way were serious and there were no clear guidelines. Friends, relatives, and associates showered the victim with unsolicited and often irrelevant advice. Some said why be a sucker, why make a fuss about it? Sign the bloody oath and forget about it. Keep the paychecks coming. Fortunately Rowe's wife agreed with his position and his father was supportive.

In retrospect, we can be proud that a handful of individuals at San Francisco State refused to sign: John Beecher, Frank Rowe, Dr. Eason Monroe, Herbert Bisno, Dr. Leonard Pockman, Lucy Hancock, Charlotte Howard, Phiz Mezey, and the long struggle to have the Levering Act set aside began. Seventeen years later the California Supreme Court ruled that the act was unconstitutional. Then more work, more petitions, more meetings, more litigation, and the same court ruled—December 30, 1971—that one of the nonsigners who had held tenure, Dr. Eason Monroe, was entitled to reinstatement, twenty-one years after he had been wrongfully discharged! Finally in 1976 the legislature adopted a resolution expressing the view that the other nonsigners should be reinstated, if they so desired, but with no provision for back pay. John Beecher, Phiz Mezey, and Frank Rowe were then reinstated, after more than a quarter century in outer darkness! More petitions and more hearings followed and then, in 1979, the State Board of Control recommended to the legislature that a token twenty-five thousand dollars award be given to each of six claimants, only fifteen percent of what they thought was their real loss.

It is really an incredible story and one that deserves to be read and re-read and pondered far into the night. In these pages you can learn about the late Earl Warren's role, of Jack Tenney's crass monkeyshines, of the pious declamations of Harold K. Levering. Also you can read about what happened to those who lost their teaching positions; there was a suicide, several divorces, one non-signer turned out to be an informer, etc.

A sorry tale; a sad commentary. And yet the record—and the memory—is redeemed by the gallant behavior of a half dozen men and women who decided to take a stand in defense of the Bill of Rights. They paid heavily for the privilege but that is all the more reason to honor them. And who knows, the legislature may yet vote funds to pay the suggested compromise awards.

This is the story of just one major episode of the McCarthy period, but it was and is—for we have not yet heard the last of it—a major chapter. It is a chapter recounted with candor, dignity, and grace; it is told as it should be told, that is, as personal history, with total authenticity.

But, for the record, may I add a footnote? Not long after Eason Monroe had been discharged at San Francisco State, the Southern California chapter of the American Civil Liberties Union was questing about for a new director. I was then a member of the board and it occcurred to me that Eason would be a fine choice and the other board members agreed. It was from this new base, in Los Angeles, that he was able to launch the long struggle to up-end the odious Levering Act.

Carey McWilliams

PREFACE

I
N THE YEARS CALLED the McCarthy era, from the late
1940s until the early 1960s, legislatures throughout the
land were obsessed with political heresy. They tried to
ferret those they saw as subversives out of every govern-
mental and political body. Prompted by the ardor of the
legislative investigating committees, the media as well as many
schools, community groups, private businesses, and social
clubs — institutions that had never before required members to
reveal their political beliefs — joined in the witch-hunt. A favorite
technique for forcing the "heretics" out in the open was to require
members, employees, or applicants to sign so-called loyalty
oaths, which forced them to reveal their political beliefs. The
idea was that those who refused to sign could be automatically
considered "disloyal," and thus dangerous.

Oaths, of course, were nothing new. Many citizens had
occasion to take the Oath of Allegiance to the United States
Constitution, some several times, upon entering the armed
forces, applying for government jobs, and so on. I had signed the
oath freely in these circumstances and was always proud to affirm
my belief in free speech. But the special oaths of the 1950s were
something else. Instead of *affirming* one's loyalty, one was *forced
to deny* membership in vaguely defined organizations. And membership in what? The Communist Party USA was specified in a
few special oaths, in spite of the fact that it is not illegal for
citizens of the United States of America to belong to that party.
But in most of the special oaths of the period, one had to guess

what was meant by this clause: ''nor am I a member of any party or organization, political or otherwise, that now advocates the overthrow of the government by force or violence.'' Again, this denial was forced upon U.S. citizens in spite of many rulings that advocacy, even of things abhorrent to the majority, is one of our constitutional rights.

Most special loyalty oaths even required the signer to swear that he or she would not become a member of unspecified organizations in the future. And there was no choice in the matter, it was either sign or get out! For many, the latter meant leaving a job of long standing. For others, it meant losing the chance to do the work they were trained for. The special oaths of the McCarthy era were clearly unconstitutional, as would eventually be proven by rulings of the highest courts in our land. Their rulings would show that an enemy among us of far greater menace than minority political parties has been the witch-hunters themselves.

This book is about one such oath, the Levering Oath, hastily written and made a requirement for all state employees by the California legislature in September 1950. The book records my personal experience as an art teacher at San Francisco State College, plus my experiences after dismissal for refusing to sign. The Levering Oath was just one of many offenses against the civil rights of the American people, but because of the features it had in common with other acts of repression in that period, its lesson is universal.

The reasons for this book? One is to clarify the nature of McCarthy era oaths. Another is to describe the fear that destroyed the unity among progressive elements in our society—a unity that has never been restored. A more general goal is to stimulate discussion. Are we any less conformist than we were in 1950? Schools have reinstated teachers who were dismissed for no other reason than the principled rejection of McCarthyite oaths, but only after protracted struggles, and even then, without financial compensation for the losses they sustained. Would teachers now resist a new wave of antiradical hysteria? I suggest that conformity may be so institutionalized today that we are no longer able to recognize it.

Finally, I hope that this book will suggest that some of the problems we face—inflation, the threat of war in the Middle East, the destruction of the environment, and the loss of confidence in democratic government—might have been less serious now, and that many of our current troubles might even have been avoided, if the teachers who could have led us in reasoned, free discussion had not been silenced.

THE OATH OF ALLEGIANCE

I, _Frank Rowe_, do solemnly swear (or affirm) that I will support and defend the Constitution of the United States and the Constitution of the State of California against all enemies, foreign and domestic; that I will bear true faith and allegiance to the Constitution of the United States and the Constitution of the State of California; that I take this obligation freely, without any mental reservation or purpose of evasion; and that I will well and faithfully discharge the duties upon which I am about to enter.

THE LEVERING OATH

And I do further swear (or affirm) that I do not advocate, nor am I a member of any party or organization, political or otherwise, that now advocates the overthrow of the Government of the United States or of the State of California by force or violence or other unlawful means; that within five years immediately preceding the taking of this oath (or affirmation) I have not been a member of any party or organization, political or otherwise, that advocated the overthrow of the Government of the United States or of the State of California by force or violence or other unlawful means except as follows: _____ (if no affiliations, write in the words "No Exceptions") and that during such time as I am a member or employee of the _____ (name of public agency) I will not advocate nor become a member of any party or organization, political or otherwise, that advocates the overthrow of the Government of the United States or of the State of California by force or violence or other unlawful means.

What we believe in waits latent forever through all the continents,
Invites no one, promises nothing, sits in calmness and light, is positive
    and composed, knows no discouragement,
Waiting patiently, waiting its time.

Walt Whitman
Leaves of Grass

Chapter 1

HUNDREDS OF SOLDIERS moved along the white-taped processing lines at a military separation center. I was there to be discharged from the army in February 1946 after the War Against Fascism. I wore my Silver Star and Purple Heart ribbons with pride. A sergeant asked if I wanted to join the inactive reserves. I hadn't given the idea a thought until that moment. My impromptu decision to sign up was aided by grumbling behind me. "You're holding up the line!" someone shouted. I thought, as I signed, that a reserve army wouldn't be needed again, at least not in my lifetime.

The civilian world I was entering differed greatly from the prewar world. During the previous summer, on June 26, 1945, at ceremonies at the San Francisco Opera House, Alger Hiss, the able Secretary General of the founding convention of the United Nations, had watched President Truman sign for the United States the charter for the organization created to preserve the peace. Only days after I became a civilian, and less than a year after the signing of the United Nations charter, British Prime Minister Winston Churchill, at a ceremony in Fulton, Missouri, declared, "Beware . . . time may be short . . . from Stettin in the Baltic to Trieste in the Adriatic, an Iron Curtain has descended across the continent."

Churchill's stentorian warning instilled a fear of the socialist bogeymen in most Americans and finished the destruction of whatever remained of the uneasy alliance between the United

States and the USSR. When I read Churchill's remarks, I recalled a conversation I had had with a German lieutenant in Opheusden, the Netherlands, in October 1944. My parachute regiment had been engaged in a bloody seesaw battle for the little town near Arnhem, and the German was one of a number of prisoners of war waiting to be moved to rear areas. We had huddled in the cellar of a bombed out house while mortar shells crashed overhead. Wounded soldiers from both sides lay next to us, moaning with pain. In excellent English, the German asked, "Why are we fighting? Soon the Germans and the Americans will be fighting side by side against the real enemy, Russia." These words had seemed crazy when the German spoke them, but in 1946, in the context of Churchill's statement, they were strangely disquieting.

Now we were entering an even crazier time. Soon conservatives would be called radicals, aggression would be known as defense, and amibitious demagogues would be hailed as saviors!

I wandered about the country for a bit, trying to calm down (I had participated in the D-day landing in France, where I had parachuted behind Utah Beach at H hour minus 5; I also served in the battle for the Arnhem Bridge and in the encirclement of Bastogne).[1] Then my wife, Marguerite, and I decided to make California our home. Certainly, a settling influence was the birth of our first daughter, Nancy, on December 1, 1946.

On our first day in San Francisco, I wore a new double-breasted civilian suit, with a tiny brass eagle emblem on the lapel. The eagle was affectionately called the "ruptured duck," and veterans wore it to show that they had served in the War Against Fascism.

Our first Bay Area home was in a public housing project, across the bay from San Francisco. We went on picnics with my sister Margery and her husband, a brewmaster who had fled Hitler's Germany. Together we saw the sights and planned our future. Marguerite worked in an office and I worked as a freight handler at the National Ice Company on San Francisco's Battery Street. I had found the job through Local 6 of the International Longshoremen and Warehousemen's Union.

After due deliberation, we decided that, since I had completed four years of liberal arts studies at the University of Oregon before the war, I should become an art teacher. I left the ice company and enrolled at San Francisco State College. A year later, I received a teaching credential in art. We moved to a two-apartment quonset hut in the student housing project; in the adjoining duplex lived fellow students Les and Mary Wright. While living there, I did practice teaching at Lowell High School and Presidio Junior High School in San Francisco.

We were busy with our personal lives, but we felt a growing sense of disenchantment as we saw people we knew and read of others making compromises with the idealism that many, ourselves included, had felt during the war. Maybe the idealism we thought we had seen had never existed at all. Reading helped us to understand that an economic system need not be immutably based on profits and that a democratic socialist economy would prob-

ably be the answer to many of our society's problems. But the
most compelling lesson in our political education was our
observation that people who expressed such heresies were being
harassed at a rapidly accelerating rate. Anything that suggested
socialism, or even simple cooperation, might be condemned. One
influential congressman even called the United Nations Educa-
tional, Scientific, and Cultural Organization (UNESCO) "the
greatest subversive plot in history."[2]

Politicians of considerably less intelligence than Winston
Churchill had taken firm control on the western side of the
symbolic barrier he had named the Iron Curtain. Representative
Richard M. Nixon, Representative J. Parnell Thomas, FBI Director J. Edgar Hoover, Senator Pat McCarran, and many others
vied to be the leading anti-Communist. And on the Soviet side
of the Iron Curtain, the grey story of the Gulag Archipelago
developed.

Marguerite and I tried to understand the reasons for the
witch-hunting. The Czechoslovakian *coup d'etat* and the Berlin
blockade provided an appropriate backdrop for the inquisitors to
develop their thesis that domestic radicals were "boring from
within." Harold Hyman, in his *To Try Men's Souls,* had one
explanation: "Many troubled Americans searched for a cause of
Russian gains and American inadequacies in the Cold War,
and found a ready reason in domestic disloyalty."[3]

While I was practice teaching at San Francisco's Lowell
High School in 1947, we read that two teachers in Hawaii had
been summarily suspended because they did not "possess the
ideals of democracy by reason of their membership in the
Communist Party." John Reinecke had taught at Honolulu's
Farrington High School and Aiko Reinecke had taught at the
Waialae Elementary School. No one had complained about either
of them.[4]

On Armistice Day, just two weeks before the Reineckes
were suspended, Governor Ingram Stainback charged that the
Communists saw Hawaii as fertile ground for the growth of their
party. Coincidentally, perhaps, the International Longshoremen
and Warehousemen's Union was then locked in a bitter struggle

with the pineapple and sugar cane industries.[5]

Just two months before the incidents in Hawaii, in August 1947, the Los Angeles County Board of Supervisors had enacted a loyalty-check program. Twenty-five county employees lost their jobs. Two court actions were filed on behalf of the heretical workers; *Parker et al.* v. *Los Angeles County* and *Steiner* v. *Darby*. The pleas of the Los Angeles County workers were dismissed by the United States Supreme Court, with Justice Felix Frankfurter delivering the opinion of the court.

An interesting feature of the Los Angeles loyalty program was its reliance on a list of 145 suspect organizations made up with the help of information furnished by the FBI, the Los Angeles Police Department "Red Squad," and other agencies. If a county worker had ever belonged to any of the organizations named, this fact was to be noted on a checklist. Examples of the organizations on the list were the Anti-ROTC Committee, the League of Women Shoppers, and the Motion Picture Cooperative Buyers Guild.

On October 14, 1948, twelve members of the national board of the Communist Party were found guilty of "conspiracy *to advocate* the violent overthrow of the government" (italics mine), and Judge Medina sentenced eleven of the defendants to five years in prison and $5,000 fines. Robert Thompson, a decorated hero in the War Against Fascism, received a three-year sentence and fine.

Perhaps the most massive breach of civil liberty came when President Truman authorized the creation of a ponderous bureau, the Loyalty Review Board, which was to screen 2 million government employees and would require hearings for each one of those suspected of disloyalty. Hundreds of employees with a cumulative total of thousands of unquestioned years of service resigned or were dismissed.

The inquisitional hysteria was fanned by a sensational investigation of the movie industry by the House Committee on Un-American Activities. Its chairman, Congressman J. Parnell Thomas (later sent to the penitentiary for padding his congressional payroll), elicited from "friendly" witnesses the names of writers and actors suspected of political heresy. Adolph Menjou, George Murphy, and Robert Taylor were a few of the "stars" who cooperated with the investigation. As president of the Screen Actors Guild, Ronald Reagan urged the witch-hunting congressmen to behave with caution, but in the same breath he expressed an abhorrence of communism.

The testimony heard by the committee was characterized by vague references and innuendoes. For example, Ginger Rogers' mother, Lila, testified to the committee that *None But the Lonely Heart* was a "film full of despair and loneliness with background music by Hanns Eisler which was moody and somber throughout, in the Russian manner." A bystander remarked, "It's a good thing Poe didn't write for the movies."

The persecution of the "Hollywood Ten," a group of writers fired by nervous producers concerned with the possible loss of box-office profits, became a familiar headline. Bertolt Brecht was not one of the Ten, but he was interrogated. In time, Charles Chaplin would flee an America gone berserk with the fear of communism. Gail Sondergard, Lillian Hellman, Lionel Stander, John Garfield, and Zero Mostel were a few of the many whose careers were damaged or destroyed.

Every newspaper was bursting with new sensations. By 1948, paid government informers Louis Budenz, Freda Utley, Elizabeth Bentley, and Whittaker Chambers — all ex-Communist Party members — recklessly fingered former comrades and innocent strangers. Harry Dexter White, Assistant Secretary of the Treasury, appeared voluntarily before the House Committee on Un-American Activities to answer unfounded charges made by Whittaker Chambers and Elizabeth Bentley. Emotionally exhausted by this ordeal, White died of a heart attack three days after his appearance before the committee.

When the distinguished black baritone and former All-American football player Paul Robeson sang before an outdoor audience at Peekskill, New York, a mob inflamed by Robeson's sympathy for the Soviet Union stoned buses and cars as they left the concert. At least 150 people were injured. The Westchester County police openly fraternized with the stone-throwing mob.

6

Congressional witch-hunters would have had us believe that many labor unions were led by traitors. The Taft-Hartley Act of 1947 (originally the Mundt-Nixon Act) also required a special test oath—that is, a loyalty oath—of union officials. The United Mine Workers and the International Typographical Union stubbornly resisted the Taft-Hartley Oath. Most unions complied rather than lose bargaining rights with the National Labor Relations Board. President Hugh Bryson of the Marine Cooks and Stewards Union and Ben Gold of the Fur Workers were convicted of perjury in connection with the Taft-Hartley Oath, when evidence showed they may have belonged to the CPUSA. Bryson went to prison. Maurice Travis, President of the Mine, Mill and Smelter Workers Union, was convicted of perjury in connection with the oath and sentenced to eight years in prison.

The most sensational incident of the Inquisition of 1948 was the Alger Hiss case. A highly publicized investigation of "Communists in government" had produced no evidence of Hiss' participation in espionage, yet government witness Whittaker Chambers gave testimony that resulted in a trial of Hiss for perjury. He was found guilty. The same scholarly civil servant who had planned the United Nations Charter ceremony in San Francisco went to prison, and Richard Nixon, the investigating committee member who had carefully led Chambers through his weird tale of national secrets buried in pumpkins, was no longer an obscure politician from Whittier, California.

The portent of the time was aptly described by Carey McWilliams:

But if circumstances require an affirmation of loyalty, they will also require investigation and surveillance. And any attempt to investigate or verify the affirmation presupposes the use of spies and informers, the services of a political police, and the existence of some Star Chamber before which suspects can be haled for questioning.[6]

In 1949, Marguerite and I noticed with particular concern that ever greater numbers of schools required teachers to disclaim membership in vaguely defined organizations. By the end of that year, special oaths would be in effect in New York, New Jersey, Maryland, Arkansas, Kansas, and Washington. What happened

7

in Washington state had particular significance for the developments that would occur in California that year.

The Washington State Fact-Finding Committee on Un-American Activities, commonly called the Canwell Committee, conducted a sensational hearing on alleged Communist influence at the University of Washington located in Seattle. The hearing featured well-publicized ex-Communist witnesses. One of these, George Hewitt, identified several professors as Communist Party members or sympathizers. Hewitt claimed that Dr. Melvin Rader, a professor of philosophy, had attended a secret school organized by the CP. Rader brought suit for perjury, but many years would pass before he would be able to prove that he had been on vacation at a mountain resort during the time he was alleged by his accuser to be at the clandestine school.

Many McCarthy-era college presidents and governing boards assumed a protective coloration in the hope that they would thus avoid the inquisitors. This futile strategem may have been in the University of Washington Regents' minds as they listened to Dean Edward Lauer read a complaint against six professors who had been called before the Canwell Committee.[7] The complaint dealt with uncooperative behavior of witnesses and with the fitness of Communists to teach. The faculty's Committee on Tenure and Academic Freedom and the American Association of University Professors had ruled that Communist Party membership was not *ipso facto* evidence of unfitness. The regents, however, disregarded the ruling and voted to uphold the complaint.

Two professors who admitted membership and one who denied membership were fired from the university without severance benefits. Three professors who testified before the committee that they had left the Communist Party voluntarily were forced to sign disclaimer oaths and placed on probation. Signing a disclaimer oath had been a Washington state requirement for some time but, until that incident, had been successfully resisted by the faculty.

The San Francisco Bay Area academic community was increasingly concerned about the University of Washington

8

incidents as they unfolded. Clearly, the hysteria engendered by the Canwell Committee was encouraging the California witch-hunters to take action. One who was undoubtedly influenced was State Senator Jack B. Tenney, who was at the peak of his power in 1949. Tenney was a long-time advocate of a special loyalty oath for all state employees, including those at the University of California.

Tenney had been a leftish president of Los Angeles Local 47, American Federation of Musicians, until he became engaged in a bitter factional dispute and was not reelected. Then he stuck his pudgy finger into the postwar political winds and felt the pronounced change from Left to Right. From that moment, anti-Communism became an obsession for him. Also, Tenney was a composer. It's difficult for me to relate the pleasant strains of "Mexicali Rose" with the threats and fulminations of this would-be Torquemada, but they did indeed come from the same man. Like many politicians of his time, Tenney observed with envy the Nixon formula for success. Nixon would imply that subversion was all about us and then attack as subversive anyone who questioned the implication.

As the 1940s closed, the mad press toward conformity affected more and more lives. It was just a matter of time before most of the states, thousands of municipalities, and countless state and administrative bodies would require special oaths of lawyers, voters, union officials, and recipients of welfare. In Indiana, professional wrestlers had to swear they wouldn't overthrow the government before they could attempt to overthrow their opponent in the ring, and in California, it would be proposed that embalmers could not perform their melancholy chore until they had been cleared!

Chapter 2

N THE HOPE THAT its initiative would forestall interference by Senator Tenney and others in the legislature,
and prompted by the example of witch-hunting in Washington and other states, the University of California
enacted a special disclaimer oath of its own.[1]

Actually, it had been University of California policy since
1940 to bar Communists from serving on the university faculty.
However, this ban had not been backed with an oath requirement.
The regents had merely stated, in their 1940 dictum, that
"membership in the Communist Party is incompatible with
membership in the faculty of a state university."

In March 1949 at a meeting of the Regents of the University
of California, President Sproul moved that the following paragraph be added to the traditional Oath of Allegiance required of
all state university employees.

I do solemnly swear (or affirm) that I do not believe in, and I am not a
member of, nor do I support any party or organization that believes in,
advocates, or teaches the overthrow of the United States Government
by force or by any illegal or unconstitutional methods; that I will support
the Constitution of the United States and the Constitution of the State of
California, and that I will faithfully discharge the duties of my office
according to the best of my ability.

The regents expressed support for President Sproul's motion
provided the disclaimer oath would follow the traditional Oath of
Allegiance. This was agreed upon and the motion was adopted.

John Francis Neylan, the dour, powerful, and able Hearst attorney, was later blamed as the principal regent in favor of oath-taking. Actually, others matched or exceeded his enthusiasm for the project. One was Regent L. Mario Giannini, President of the Bank of America, who had even called for vigilante action against suspected Communists.

On June 24, 1949, after long hours of committee work, resolutions, and discussion, the oath was revised to make it more specific. This phrase was included: "that I am not a member of the Communist Party, or under any oath, or a party to any agreement, or under any commitment that is in conflict with my obligations under this oath."

The June 1949 events brought down the wrath of much of the UC faculty: Edward C. Tolman, professor of psychology, and other distinguished teachers announced that they would not sign the new oath. During the summer, more teachers refused to sign. The summer of 1949 passed with efforts at resistance and claims and counterclaims of the number who had submitted. It was announced that contracts for the 1949–50 academic year could not be completed until the oaths were signed.

A story appearing in the San Francisco *Examiner* on June 24, 1949, gave an inkling of the level of disruption that had been reached:

The faculty of the University of California will urge the Board of Regents today to drop its insistence on faculty members signing non-Communist oaths. When the Board of Regents recently proposed a non-Communist oath, not only for faculty members but for all salaried employees of the university, the Academic Senate voted almost unanimously for deletion or revision of the oath.

The regents set October 1 as the deadline for signing of all oaths. On that day, President Sproul announced that 57 percent of the faculty had signed. Then began a long period of threats, new deadlines, resignations, and attempted compromises. On April 21, 1950, a "compromise" was reached by which the oath requirement was transferred to the annual contract. Refusal to sign would not mean automatic dismissal, at least not until after a hearing before the Faculty Committee on Privilege and Tenure.

Regent Giannini resigned from the board in protest, saying, "I feel sincerely that if we rescind this oath, flags will fly from the Kremlin!"

Governor Earl Warren was an ex officio member of the Board of Regents. His reputation as an advocate of civil rights was earned at a later date, after he became Chief Justice of the United States Supreme Court. Until 1950, his civil rights record was ambivalent at best, and his worst positions were downright appalling. For example, in 1942, as attorney general of California, Warren had urged that Japanese-Americans be interned as posing imminent danger to our wartime defenses. During the national election campaign of 1948, he assailed the Progressive Party. Of the party's presidential candidate, Henry Wallace, who

had served as secretary of agriculture and vice president in the administrations of Franklin Delano Roosevelt and as secretary of commerce under President Truman, Warren said, "No, I do not say that Mr. Wallace is a Communist. I do not insinuate that he is. But I do say that leftist organizations that are attuned to the Communist movement have chosen him to muddy the political waters in our state."[2]

At still another point in Warren's career, he had opposed the repeal of a measure that excluded the Communist Party from the ballot in California. As a member of the Board of Regents, Warren often sided with the faculty in opposing the oath, but he supported the objective of the oath, the elimination of Communist faculty members. In one speech, he said, "I would cut my right arm off before I would willingly submit my youngsters to the wiles or infamy of a Communist faculty."

On June 23, 1950, with Governor Warren chairing the meeting, the regents accepted President Sproul's report recommending the "compromise." Under this plan, non-Communist Academic Senate members who had conscientious scruples against signing could be cleared by the Faculty Committee on Privilege and Tenure. The "compromise" did not apply to 157 other employees, however, who were fired. Then, at a meeting on August 25, the regents reneged on the compromise plan, and 31 members of the Academic Senate were also fired.

There is no way to determine precisely how many resignations were caused by the University of California Regents' Oath but not announced as such. Nor can we know how many classes were suspended for lack of qualified teachers, how many appointments were refused, or how many emotional and physical breakdowns resulted from the turmoil. It is certain that a number of distinguished teachers refused appointments.

The destruction of morale among academics was perhaps the most serious damage done. Alexander Meiklejohn, the civil libertarian and former President of Amherst and former Chairman of the Experimental College at the University of Wisconsin, expressed a sentiment felt increasingly by more and more people:

What were these faculty men saying about academic freedom, the

13

signers with compromise, the nonsigners without compromise? They were, I think, expressing the conviction that an institution which limits intellectual freedom is not a university. They knew that a man who assumes the social responsibilities of a scholar, a teacher, a preacher, must first of all establish, in the minds of the people whom he serves, the assurance, the certainty, that his beliefs, his utterances, are, independently, his own. They must be sure that he is a man whom no one, not even themselves, can compel to believe this or to say that, can forbid to believe that or to say this. Anyone who submits, under pressure, to coercive control over his thought or his speech, ceases to be a scholar searching for the truth, ceases to be a teacher leading his pupils toward honest and fearless inquiry and belief. He becomes a hired man, thinking what he is paid to think, saying what he is hired to say.[3]

I heard about the University of California events in my first paid teaching position, as art and crafts instructor at the San Francisco Juvenile Detention Center. My recollection of the old center at 150 Otis Street is of dirty yellow paint, papers and rubbish in the gutters, and grey bars over the windows. I can still hear the noise. The rumble of trucks going to and from the warehouses and factories in our neighborhood constantly filtered into our basement classroom.

My classes were brought to the basement by a guard even though most of the boys were there not for criminal reasons but because they had merely had the misfortune to be born into families that could not care for them. The room was kept locked from the outside, and the guard would return at the end of the work period. I had a telephone but there were fewer disciplinary problems than in the traditional high schools where I had done my student teaching. The young wards were grateful to do something other than sit in their cells.

I continued to teach at the "Juvy" in the first months of 1950. Socially useful as it might have been, teaching art under those circumstances was not what I wanted to do indefinitely. I was pleased then when Seymour Locks, an art instructor at San Francisco State College, visited my class one day to ask if I would be interested in a part-time job at the college.

Seymour was about thirty years old. Soulful dark eyes complemented his gentle face. He had studied and taught art at

14

San Jose State College and at Stanford University before being
appointed to the San Francisco State staff. He was an energetic
painter, an expressive draftsman, and a skilled lettering artist.
Students enjoyed Seymour's classes and he seemed to enjoy his
students. They often visited with him and his wife Fay at their
studio home in San Francisco's Bayview district.

Seymour suggested that I make an appointment with
Dr. J. Fenton McKenna, then Dean of the Division of Creative
Arts. I discovered when I did so that Seymour had already
recommended me.

Dr. McKenna was a friendly, open-faced man in a conservative grey suit, full of enthusiasm for the growing creative arts
curricula at the college. The interview went well. I would be hired
for the fall semester and my specific assignment would be determined by the art department chairman.

Marguerite and I had already thought seriously about the
possibility that I would be confronted with the special loyalty
oath. At the time of my interview, the oath was being imposed in
schools all over the land. Only recently, we had read about the
summary dismissal of teachers in New York City who had refused
to sign. The incident began with one teacher being summoned
before his superintendent. The superintendent demanded, "Are
you now, or were you ever, a member of the Communist Party?"
The teacher didn't answer. He and seven others were dismissed
for refusing to answer the question. The school rationalized the
action by describing the teachers' behavior as "insubordination
and conduct unbecoming a teacher." The teachers involved
vowed to go to the highest court; in the meantime, they were
blacklisted. Soon after we read of this incident, a page-one
story ran in the San Francisco *Examiner* topped by the ominous
headline, "Oath Asked in Colleges — State Probers Seek Test
of Employees."

Our second daughter, Patricia, had been born with a defect
that eventually led to her death in 1951. Aside from the emotional
strain the illness placed on us, our expenses were greatly
increased by medical bills. Marguerite and I agreed that the
offer by San Francisco State might lead to a rewarding future,

15

even though the political climate was deteriorating.

I looked forward to a return to my alma mater with mixed feelings. If a special political test oath was to be imposed in California, I did have the option, of course, to sign and continue with my work, but without a clear conscience. No matter what harm might be done to individual careers, including mine, freedom of expression would be the real casualty. Any unorthodoxy would be expressed less openly than before, if at all. Anyone with a slightly heretical bent, such as ourselves, who had ever expressed the thought that capitalism might not be the beginning and end of everything ideal forever, or who had ever harbored the notion that America and capitalism might not be synonymous, would be marked.

The event that brought anti-Communist hysteria to a fever pitch and made a special oath for all California public employees a virtual certainty was the war in Korea. We were visiting my father in Oregon on Sunday, June 25, 1950, the day the war started.

When he was a young man, my father had opened a bank in an Oregon coastal town and had represented the community in the state legislature. His bank failed after a "run" caused by a change of plan by the railroad, which had led businessmen to believe that a main line would go through the area. After the bank debacle, my father developed a specialty lumber business, but that failed in the Great Depression. In old age, he broke his precept against working for a salary, and when we visited in 1950, he was employed by the Jackson County Farmer's Committee to administer applications for subsidy payments from the federal government.

One evening during our visit, he told us about an encounter he had had with Lila Rogers, movie star Ginger's mother, who had told alarming tales of "communism" in Hollywood as a witness at the 1948 hearings of the House Un-American Activities Committee. The Rogers owned a show ranch on the bank of Oregon's beautiful Rogue River. My father had helped them get subsidy payments from the government even as they bemoaned the decline of "free enterprise." At a public hearing, Lila had declared that his work with the farmer's committee was "socialistic."

Incredible to hear my father accused of socialism! He had spent most of his life trying to succeed in the laissez faire mold. But that little incident didn't end as Lila Rogers may have intended. Even conservative Oregonians recognized the absurdity of her charge, and my father gained a perception of things as they were. He joked, "Owners scream 'socialism' if a migratory worker remains in the county one day after the last pear has been picked, but they're in the office for a handout when prices fall."

Marguerite, our little daughter Nancy, and I returned to San Francisco in mid-July. Headlines about the war in Korea had almost buried the story of a certain ex-sergeant, David Greenglass, who had been stationed at the Los Alamos atomic weapons laboratory. Greenglass was the brother of Ethel Rosenberg. Later, the trial of Ethel and Julius Rosenberg, who were betrayed to the FBI by the terrified Greenglass, would become the most sensational espionage story in U.S. history.

The case involving *Amerasia* magazine was also pushed off the front pages by the war. The editors of the magazine, which was funded by Frederick Vanderbilt Field, a millionaire backer of liberal causes, had urged limited wartime collaboration between Chiang Kai-shek and the Chinese Communists. The magazine had become a favorite target for Senator McCarthy and for a Senate Committee, chaired by Senator Millard Tydings, charged with investigating Communists in the State Department.

The United Nations Security Council adopted a U.S. resolution demanding withdrawal of the North Koreans, thus permitting our government to call the war a "police action," one of the many euphemisms of the fifties and sixties designed to obscure the motives of our hawkish leaders.

As we feared, the Korean War strengthened the hand of the University of California Regents in the year-old oath controversy. On July 22, the San Francisco *Examiner* reported, "Regents Meet to Consider Impasse . . . 20 of 62 who refused have reconsidered." Details followed: "Among the new signers were some of the leaders of the rebellion against the anti-Communist pledge. Their example, coupled with the unmasking of the international Communist intent by the Korean invasion, is expected to signal the end of the anti-pledge movement."

The very words of the Hearst reporter, "unmasking of the international Communist intent," added more fuel to the hysteria. Heretics who were foolhardy enough to dispute the official explanation of the events of June 25 were denounced as traitors.

Many people believed, but almost no one said, that the pretext of the war—the crossing of the 38th Parallel by the North Koreans—had been provoked. They noted the strange coincidence of a visit to the frontline positions by John Foster Dulles, the contentious U.S. Secretary of State, just one day before the "invasion."

My father had wanted us to stay in Oregon. He advised us not to become involved in the anti-Communist hysteria. To him, espionage stories, Red-baiting, and even the new war in Korea seemed a long way from Oregon's pine trees and clear streams. Marguerite and I have often wondered how things might have turned out if we had taken his advice.

Chapter 3

AS THE SUMMER of 1950 waned, Marguerite and I kept hoping that nothing would happen to prevent my return to San Francisco State as a teacher at the beginning of the fall semester. My summer of 1950 was climaxed by an opportunity to study painting with Max Beckmann at Mills College. I was more familiar with the story of his exile from Nazi Germany than with his pictures. He had been a recognized painter, graphic artist, and teacher in Frankfurt. Because of Beckmann's pictures, which the Nazis had branded "degenerate," and not because of his race, he and his wife, Quappi, were forced to flee Germany. The German Fascists despised modern artists with almost the same ferocity with which they hated the Jews. After leaving Germany, the Beckmanns lived in Holland, and, when the Fascists made their lives intolerable there, they fled to southern France. A bit later, they emigrated to this country.

Mills is a small, privately endowed, liberal arts women's college. Its mixture of Victorian and Spanish-style buildings is spaciously arranged amidst lawns and trees, a world apart from the nearby sprawl of shopping centers and freeways. At that time, the college was well known for its summer workshops. They were open to men as well as women, and artists came from all over the United States to attend. Before Beckmann, Fernand Leger and Yasuo Kuniyoshi had been guest teachers.

That summer, Seymour Locks, my friend from San Francisco State, also attended Beckmann's class. We arranged to ride together, taking Locks' car and mine on alternate days.

Beckmann looked almost as he had portrayed himself in his paintings. In some, he had worn a tuxedo and formal collar. In our class, he usually wore a lightweight cardigan, grey slacks, and a conservative necktie. He had a heavy physique but without the appearance of obesity. His self-portraits had led me to think he would be gruff, so I was surprised by his pleasant voice and the humorous sparkle in his eyes. If I had met him on the street without prior acquaintance, I might have mistaken him for a judge or perhaps a professor of history.

Quappi always accompanied Beckmann in class, since she translated criticism that he could phrase only in German. Before the class, I hadn't considered Beckmann's color one of his strengths, but an exhibition of his paintings in the Mills gallery that summer gave me an appreciation, which even the finest photograph cannot, of the sometimes dissonant but always expressive color combinations behind the black framework of his compositions.

The principal value of the class, however, was the example Beckmann set. I have never known anyone with such a complete and uncompromising determination to express himself in spite of

every material or political obstacle.

On the last day of the summer session, the students gave a party for Beckmann and Quappi at the home of Dr. Hedley, the Mills chaplain. Baked salmon and vodka were served, Beckmann's choice. Beckmann took his vodka straight. When Seymour offered him a drink with soda and a celery stick, he refused, remarking, "No vegetables, thank you."

After the party, Marguerite and I returned to San Francisco with Seymour and Fay Locks and we talked about what we had learned during the course. I remember saying that Beckmann had taught me that the masters of impressionism, post-impressionism, cubism, futurism, expressionism, and dadaism were able to create for the very reason that they were outside the moribund esthetic, economic, and political systems. I found that thought stimulating in light of current political developments: I was coming to see that repression might possibly force me to work from an alienated position similar to conditions those artists had known.

San Franciscans enjoyed typical fall weather in September 1950. Cooling fog from the ocean would blanket the city in the early morning, retreat by midday, and then push over Twin Peaks

again as evening approached. In the Mission District, where we had moved, the weather characteristically stayed sunny and warm much longer than in any other part of the city because of intervening hills and air currents.

Our home was the upper flat of a "carpenter Gothic" style house on Alabama Street. We rented it for $35 a month when Karl Kasten, an instructor at San Francisco State College, left to take a new post at the university in Berkeley. Mrs. Mohr, in the downstairs flat, was Karl's aunt and our landlady. That plump, tidy German woman showed us a nearby house that marked the limit of the catastrophic 1906 fire. Everything south of Market Street to that very house had burned after the earthquake.

The living and dining room walls of our high-ceilinged flat curved near the ceiling. The lower part of the curve was trimmed with an ornate Victorian motif. Our fireplace was bordered with aqua tile. We rented a tiny backyard from the church on the corner where Marguerite and Nancy could plant a few flowers.

On the first day of the fall semester and my first day as an instructor, I drove our 1942 Studebaker two-door sedan (a rare model because automobile factories had converted to tank and other war-material production in 1942). The college had no

parking lot, but I found a spot a few blocks from the campus.
I knew I wouldn't be late because nervousness about a first day
has always compelled me to be in my classroom, fussing with
paper, easels, and other incidentals of teaching, at least an
hour before the bell.

The campus occupied a large city block, bounded by Haight,
Buchanan, Hermann, and Laguna Streets. From this hillside
location one could see the upper Market Street area, City Hall,
and the downtown skyline.

The 5,249 students at San Francisco State that fall came
from all socioeconomic levels, although more students were from
working-class families than would have been the case at most
four-year colleges. The tuition was reasonable and many students
lived at home. Moreover, more than a thousand of the students
were veterans, a large number were married, and many held
part-time jobs.

The college cafeteria was the most popular meeting place.
A corner drugstore and two nearby restaurants were other social
centers. Coca-Cola, soft drinks, or coffee were the favorites, but
if anyone wanted a glass of beer after class there were bars nearby
on Market Street. Most of us couldn't believe the rumor that some
students used marijuana. Until then, only swing drummer Gene
Krupa and "dope fiends" were known to have used it.

Even with the shortage of social facilities, San Francisco
State College at the start of that fall semester was friendly,
informal, and democratic. Johnny Mathis was to be the most
famous alumnus of the class of 1950.

My classes got off to a good start. Beginning a new semester
has always reminded me of push-starting a car. If enough momen-
tum is gained early enough, the instructor can stand aside and let
things happen. If not, the teacher must push and push and perhaps
never get it going.

After class that first day, I enjoyed coffee and conversation
with some students in the cafeteria. The news stories and editorials in the first fall issue of the *Golden Gater*,[1] the college
newspaper, quickly became the subjects of our conversation. The
lead editorial made this philosophical observation: "Season

follows season. And what to expect . . . you can never tell."

I was so preoccupied with the opening of the fall semester in the first weeks of September that I hardly read a newspaper. If I had, I would have noticed that Governor Warren had called a special session of the legislature to strengthen the civil defenses of California.

Students and teachers had settled into the rhythm of the new semester. A story appeared in the *Gater* about plans for homecoming, including the coronation of a queen, and the "Block S" dance. We read about Joe Verducci's football team. The Gaters, under the tutelage of their outstanding coach and with a larger than average percentage of black athletes, were expected to win many games. However, the *Gater* reporter warned that the games with the Chico Wildcats and with Southern Oregon College would be very close.

Elsewhere in the college newspaper there was an announcement that the Freddy Martin band of Hollywood Coconut Grove fame, would conduct tryouts in the music department. A few students would have an opportunity to play with the famous band.

Then, on September 25, the calamity that Marguerite and I had excruciated over for untold hours occurred! The newspapers announced that the state legislature had passed, and Governor Warren had signed into law, an act sponsored by Assemblyman Levering to strengthen our civil defenses and to amend the sabotage-prevention act.

Harold K. Levering was a member of the California legislature from the Los Angeles area (Santa Monica) and had owned a large Chevrolet dealership before getting into politics. For some time he had felt ordained to save the state, especially its schools, from being destroyed from within. Now, with Governor Warren's call for a speedy overhaul of the security system, he had his big chance! He had composed a loyalty oath, and by the time a few other Red-baiting politicians *and* Governor Warren had added penalties and other final touches, they decided to call it the Levering Act. It was so good, they thought, that it should apply to anyone who received so much as a thin dime from the state—

HAROLD K. LEVERING

from artists' models and bus drivers to college presidents. Not only that, but according to the law every public worker would be drafted as a civil defense worker.

San Francisco State College was not to be spared, as I and my colleagues were to learn.

It was not hard to understand Governor Warren's motives in urging the Levering Act on the legislature. He was in a difficult campaign for a third term as governor, facing James Roosevelt, the eldest son of FDR. Roosevelt had criticized the Truman Doctrine, thus alienating many conservative Democrats. Roosevelt's criticism had also angered Truman, who would not endorse his candidacy. It was clear that Earl Warren was trying to woo the disenchanted conservative Democrats into his camp.

- Earlier, conservative Democrats and Republican regulars had threatened to throw their support to Lieutenant Governor Goodwin Knight in his candidacy for governor. This move was thwarted when Governor Warren publicly announced his third-term candidacy, but Warren was more and more anxious to establish his anti-Communist credentials. Just before the special legislative session, he made these remarks to a convention of Disabled American Veterans:

For there are those who, woefully misguided or insane, find some psychopathic satisfaction in betraying their country. There are others who had been and will be carefully placed to sabotage our industry, our communications, our transportation, and against these loathsome apostles of deceit and destruction, we must guard our land, our people, and our homes.[2]

Warren made this inflammatory speech in the full knowledge that no sabotage of industry, destruction of communications, or violence whatsoever had occurred.

The new law was discussed on campus at a general faculty meeting the day after its passage. I first read the exact language in a hastily prepared mimeographed handout.[3] It was true! All public employees were now "civil defense workers subject to such civilian defense activities as may be assigned to them by their superiors or by law." The implications of that development were menacing enough, but the oath itself was my immediate concern.

The first paragraph of the new pledge was the same oath that all public employees had taken for many years, the same positive statement of allegiance to the Constitution that I had willingly signed when I served in the army, when I was employed by the juvenile court, and, again, when I was employed by San Francisco State College. The second paragraph contained the new language. It required that the public employee disclaim certain beliefs, an absolute contradiction of the constitutional guarantees of free speech and assembly that one swore to support and defend in the original oath. The exact words were these:

And I do further swear (or affirm) that I do not advocate, nor am I a member of any party or organization, political or otherwise, that now advocates the overthrow of the Government of the United States or of the State of California by force or violence or other unlawful means; that within five years immediately preceding the taking of this oath (or affirmation) I have not been a member of any party or organization, political or otherwise, that advocated the overthrow of the Government of the United States or of the State of California by force or violence or other unlawful means except as follows: _____ (If no affiliations, write in the words "No Exceptions") and that during such time as I am a member or employee of the _____ _____ (name of public agency) I will not advocate nor become a member of any party or organization, political or otherwise, that advocates the overthrow of the Government of the United States or of the State of California by force or violence or other unlawful means.

Since I had been at the college for only three weeks, I was acquainted with only a few people at the meeting. But it was apparent that the person who spoke with the greatest feeling against the new oath was a thin and slightly stooped man whose suit seemed a bit too large and whose necktie was slightly awry. His slightly rumpled appearance was soon forgotten, however, because of his intense speech.

Seymour Locks, seated next to me, identified him as Dr. Leonard Pockman, an associate professor of physics. Seymour said that Pockman had taught at the college for several years and that he was very well liked by his students and his colleagues. Dr. Pockman urged unity. He said that if everyone would refuse to sign the obviously unconstitutional oath, the state would have to reconsider. It was apparent, however, that such solid oppositon would not develop. The majority of the faculty members at the meeting did not express themselves. A few teachers even expressed support for the negative oath.

A man who identified himself as a business teacher questioned Dr. Pockman: "Leonard, I don't see what all the fuss is about. I don't advocate the violent overthrow of the government and I guess you don't either." He and a few others laughed. "Why don't we just sign this thing and get on with it?"

In reply, Dr. Pockman outlined the recent history of the

27

suppression of ideas. He said it was the congressional investigating committees, police agencies, and headline-hunting politicians that determined which organizations supposedly advocated force and violence and which supposedly did not. "If the right to make such definitions is in their hands, how can anyone be safe?" he argued. He concluded by asking his questioner whether acts of violence had occurred and whether he thought they were likely enough to occur, especially on our peaceful campus, to warrant this tampering with the constitutional guarantees of free speech and assembly.

Lively conversations continued after the meeting. The vagueness of the new law was a principal concern. One woman said she had once belonged to the American League for Peace and Democracy, a group that had appeared on someone's list of alleged Communist-front organizations. Was the League an organization that advocated force and violence, according to the new oath? The Communist Party had supported the League program, and it was believed that many active Communists had belonged to it. No one could advise her. If she signed the oath without listing the organization and a Congressional Committee found that it *did* advocate the overthrow of the government by force and violence, she would be subject to prosecution for perjury. The penalty provision of the new law was clear. Upon conviction of perjury, one could be sentenced to a state prison for not less than one year nor more than fourteen years.

This woman's alternative, however, might be self-incrimination. If, to be safe from perjury charges, she listed the organization, she ran the risk of prosecution under any of several laws that had been in use since the start of the McCarthy inquisition: the Federal Smith Act, the State Criminal Syndicalism Act, or the Subversive Organization Registration Law of California. The recently enacted McCarran Act was the most sinister possibility.

The McCarran Act, sponsored by the Senator from Nevada, required any organization associated with Communists to register with the government.[4] The act contained ominous provisions for the holding of alleged subversives in detention camps without the

28

right of habeas corpus. This meant that police agencies might throw people into the camps without even bringing them before a court. The McCarran Act was passed by the United States Congress on September 12, 1950. It was vetoed by President Truman, but Congress quickly overrode the veto. Congressional approval of the McCarran Act spurred the California legislature and local governments into even more zealous witch-hunting.

In still more after-meeting conversation, teachers expressed outrage at the role of Governor Warren. "Didn't he oppose the special oath at the University of California?" someone asked. "That he talked out of both sides of his mouth is closer to the truth," was the reply. I threw in my opinion: "Now he has signed a more repressive law for *all* public employees. Don't forget that we've been conscripted as 'civil defense workers.' That has never before been a part of loyalty-oath proposals. And all of this without a single public hearing!"

We agreed that Governor Warren had obviously decided that opposing loyalty oaths was a luxury he could no longer afford. Now he had switched to a position of open sponsorship. In short, his accommodation to practical politics was only too apparent.

I needed to refresh my memory about some of the terms used at the meeting, so I stopped at the college library where I made comparisons among some terms used in the Levering Act, the U.S. Constitution, and dictionary definitions.

The new oath mandated that "all public employees are hereby declared to be civil defense workers subject to such civilian defense activities as may be assigned to them by their superiors." It seemed to me that the constitutional phrase, "nor involuntary servitude, except as a punishment for crime whereof the party shall have been duly convicted, shall exist within the United States, or any place subject to their jurisdiction" was intended to prevent the very thing the oath proposed.

Article I, Section 10 of the Constitution states, "No state shall pass any bill of attainder, ex post facto law, or law impairing the obligation of contracts." Webster's definition of *ex post facto* is, "any law enacted with retrospective effect." *Bill of attainder* is defined as "extinction of the civil rights and capacities of a person." Clearly, the Levering Oath phrase "within the five years immediately preceding the taking of this oath" was *ex post facto* and all of the restraints imposed by the oath constituted a *bill of attainder*.

The Fifth Amendment of the Constitution clearly states that one cannot "be compelled in any criminal case to be a witness against himself . . .," and yet the Levering Oath would force teachers to list organizations that might later be used against them. The Fourteenth Amendment provision for due process was also obviously in contradiction to the Levering Oath phrase, "No compensation nor reimbursement for expenses incurred shall be paid to any civil defense worker by any public agency unless such civil defense worker has taken and subscribed to the oath . . . ."

I went to my mailbox after I left the library. There was the damnable oath, in the middle of a mass of mimeographed bulletins, paper-clipped to a memorandum from the business office. The latter urged all staff members to sign the oath as soon as possible. Any delay, it warned, might prevent prompt delivery of November paychecks!

Chapter 4

I T WAS IMPOSSIBLE TO DECIDE whether or not to sign at that moment. I decided to discuss my dilemma with other teachers, with Marguerite and perhaps with a lawyer.

October 1950 was indeed a period of soul-searching for many at San Francisco State College. Everyone subject to the new oath was required to sign by midnight, November 2. Included were all who received money from the state, no matter how minor the position or how paltry the amount. Several things happened that month in the outside world that may have influenced our decisions.

Following the amphibious landing at Inchon, General Douglas MacArthur's United Nations-approved American Army pushed across Korea's 38th Parallel. Apparently President Truman was worried. On October 9, MacArthur issued a second surrender ultimatum to the North Koreans, which was ignored. President Truman announced that he would fly to an island in the Pacific Ocean for a conference.

On his way to the Wake Island conference with his head-strong commander, Truman stopped off in the Bay Area, where he made a speech and conferred with Governor Warren. After their conversation, Warren said that he was "happy to be able to inform President Truman that we responded immediately to his call for civil defense in California." He said that California was "now building, stone by stone, with the Government" in that

31

department. This brought a picture to my mind of Liberty under the stones, which I translated into a poster for the International Relations Club.

On October 25, the Chinese entered the war, which resulted in a nearly disastrous retreat by MacArthur's troops in the freezing cold. The American people, with the possible exception of Harry Truman, found it hard to believe that the hero of Bataan could be in such deep military trouble.

In general, the country was prosperous. "Defense" industries provided many jobs. Air Force General Emmett O'Donnell called the Korean War "a made-to-order situation to keep business on a high level."

That year, diversion from reverses in Korea and from the hysterical snooping into people's personal histories was offered by movie stars and by "non-controversial" television shows. Would Ava Gardner's marriage to Frank Sinatra last? Would color television be a reality in the near future? Not likely in either case. "You Bet Your Life" with Groucho Marx and Bert Parks'

"Stop the Music" were favorites. The cover of *Life* magazine featured Ed Wynn with the caption, "TV Gets Top Comics." Radio and television executives used *Red Channels*, a handbook written by ex-FBI agents, to identify "subversives" in entertainment. They were cautioned against hiring Edward G. Robinson, Orson Welles, and Gypsy Rose Lee, among many others.

People found further diversion in sports events. A thirty-six-year-old Joe Louis had just been clobbered by Ezzard Charles in a world's championship boxing match. In the fifth game of the baseball World Series, the New York Yankees' Yogi Berra hit a home run that launched a winning three-run drive against Philadelphia, ending the series 3 to 2 in favor of the Yankees. Some citizens enjoyed the series over radios in new cars with Hydramatic, Powerglide, Starlight windows, and other innovations.

Still, children huddled under desks in daily air-raid drills. New York City approved a $400 million plan for the construction of shelters under city parks and playgrounds. Suburban real estate salespeople offered easy-pay plans on backyard bomb shelters.

October 1950, then, was not a time for the expression of unpopular ideas or for the defense of heretics. In spite of the absence of *real* violence or subversion, our political leaders had convinced most people that almost anything could happen, from atomic bomb attack to invasion of our coastline.

The International Relations Club, a student organization dedicated to a search for understanding between nations (personal letters to students behind the Iron Curtain was a favorite project) became the sponsor of the first real discussion of the oath.

The college administration had denied students the use of campus facilities for discussion of the subject, even though the International Relations Club was a properly constituted student organization. So the students went to the nearby Unitarian Church, which offered them a room. When I think back to this incident, with a knowledge of the rebellion of American youth in the 1960s, it is hard to believe that such a well-behaved group as the San Francisco State International Relations Club could have been denied the use of a campus hall. But such was the fear-laden

33

nature of the time.

The Reverend Harry Meserve had already delivered a lucid indictment of special oath-taking in a Sunday sermon.[1] There he made the following remarks:

Now, if this is what loyalty really is . . .not conformity to particular policies or theories of political or economic life but fidelity to the principles and aims of individual liberty, equal justice, and human brotherhood for which a government claims to stand, we must face a very searching question about our own time. Who is really disloyal in this deepest sense? Is it, for example, Owen Lattimore, who frankly disagrees with our foreign policy toward Red China and says so fearlessly? Or is it Senator McCarthy, who, under the cloak of congressional immunity, slanders and libels Lattimore and makes a travesty of democracy by using every trick of publicity and political expediency in order to discredit the policy of his own government?

The Unitarian congregation had given Reverend Meserve rapt attention. He went on:

Is it the people who oppose the teachers' oath and refuse to sign because they believe in freedom of thought and expression, or the people who, in seeking an external conformity of all men to present policies, insist that they must sign the oath?

The point is that the demand for external conformity is in itself un-American and disloyal to the best ideals and the deepest experiences of the American people themselves. We have always known and been proud of the fact that in America men think and speak, write and assemble together as conscience and inclination dictate. And we have done this traditionally without fear of government reprisals and with a healthy sense of the dignity and power of using our minds freely. This fact is perhaps our most significant claim to greatness; and the American experience to date has been, by and large, the discovery that men of goodwill can disagree without demanding conformity and can be loyal to the highest principles of freedom and the sternest demands of the common life without believing that the government in power is the best possible one or that the prevailing policies are wholly right.

Reverend Meserve's sermon was mimeographed by the students and really started things rolling! The students billed their gathering as a "Rally for Academic Freedom." At the meeting, four teachers told the students their reasons for opposing the oath. Dr. Leonard Pockman, Associate Professor of Physics, Dr. Eason Monroe, Chairman of the Division of Language Arts, and Herbert Bisno, Assistant Professor of Sociology, all presented excellent arguments against the oath. But it was John Beecher, Assistant Professor of Sociology, who brought the students to their feet with thunderous applause when he announced that he would refuse to sign the oath!

Beecher was descended from the family of Harriet Beecher Stowe and Henry Ward Beecher. In the Depression years, he had been an administrator of government programs for the rural poor in the South. Later, he was an officer on the *Booker T. Washington*, the only Liberty ship with a black captain in the War Against Fascism. Proud and erect, his head topped with prematurely white hair, Beecher held our attention not only with his appearance, but with his incisive ideas and strong language.

I was reminded of John Brown as Beecher spoke. He had the same clear perception of the issue at hand and the determination to

commit the necessary deed, no matter the personal loss. He was the first person at State to announce, in unequivocal terms, that he would defy the oath. "I am not going to sign this oath! Your education is at stake and I think it's your fight, too. I hope you will help me to make this fight effective, memorable, and maybe pretty spectacular," he added, confidently.

Two men in business suits at the back of the room whispered to each other and one made notes.

I wasn't surprised when the International Relations Club at the college was suspended by the Student Board of Directors for sponsoring the "Rally for Academic Freedom" at the church.[2] The college administration and the docile student board named as a second offense the release of details of the controversial rally to the San Francisco newspapers!

Jack Trodden, a handsome married veteran in his senior year, was president of the IRC that year. His serious yet affable manner made him a respected campus leader. In statements to the *Golden Gater* and elsewhere, Trodden tried to assure everyone that the rally had merely been a group of interested students and faculty and in no way represented the college. The club was reinstated after a series of conferences with administration.

In a second statement, the IRC leaders did not condemn the frightened college administration for suspending the club. Instead, with reasoning characteristic of the McCarthy era, they said opposition to the new loyalty oath sprang from a concern that sinister forces threatened us. "Communists have always thrived when dissension, distrust and disunity prevail. They have made their largest gains when faction opposes faction, group opposes group, and individual opposes individual. It is our contention that this law, passed during the heat of insecurity and world conflict, strengthens the Reds' hand."

The chastised International Relations Club took no further stand against the oath, but a new, unauthorized student organization was formed called the Student Committee for Academic Freedom, or SCAF. For the rest of October, and even after the deadline for signing had passed, SCAF was the most vocal campus group opposing the new oath. Jack Trodden, Jerry Stoll,

Allen Ohta, Betty Silverman, Orville Wycoff, Bill Cather, Leonard Beecher, Joan Stuck, Erika Reimer-Wernham, Jim Bosch, Kurt Levi and Jim Wood were a few of the leaders of SCAF and editors of the SCAF *Newsletter*. Wood was not only active in SCAF but has, over the years, lent his not inconsiderable talents as a guitarist and folksinger to many popular causes.[3]

On campus and at home, we talked constantly about the new oath. We discussed social, art, and athletic events too, but bonfire rallies, Freddy Martin band tryouts, homecoming preparations, and the latest exhibitions of the à la vogue Abstract Expressionist artists seemed unreal as I tried to decide if I would sign the obviously unconstitutional oath. Of course, I had known that this crisis was coming and had long ago determined the right course. But it was not easy to do the right thing, to resist, once the crisis was upon me. Except for postermaking, I completely set aside my painting and work in graphics.

A bizarre note, in the midst of this wholesale sacking of the Bill of Rights and academic freedom, was a national "Freedom Bell" crusade, the notion of General Lucius Clay, who had been the American commander in Germany during the Berlin blockade. Specifically, the idea was to collect as many signatures as possible to show the people of West Berlin that the United

States supported them. L. Mario Giannini, President of the Bank of America and former University of California regent, was the San Francisco chairman of this patriotic event. An instructor at the college was one of a number of San Francisco coordinators. That instructor had stated that he could see no threat in the new oath. He would be proud to wrap bandages or whatever else was required in his new role as "civil defense worker."

A papier-maché bell, patterned after the historic Liberty Bell in Philadelphia and with an American flag as a backdrop, was prominently displayed in the main building at State. In front of the bell was a "Declaration of Freedom" resting on a field of red, white, and blue satin. The declaration was heavy with references to the Red tyrannies that threatened to overwhelm us. Posters announced that the bell and the declaration, with as many signatures as could be obtained, would be shipped to the citizens of West Berlin.

The display was not far from the business office. One afternoon, as I stood and watched for a few minutes, I saw several instructors go into the business office. I assumed they were signing the new oath. On their way out, they paused before the "Freedom Bell" and signed the declaration. How inspired by patriotism they must have been!

As of October 15, John Beecher was still the only teacher who had said publicly that he wouldn't sign. Other teachers had expressed disapproval of the loyalty oath, more as a protestation of their liberal credentials, it seemed to me, than as an indication of the way they would act on November 2. A "Committee of Ten,"[4] selected by the faculty, was authorized to investigate the implications of the oath and to issue a question-and-answer sheet for the guidance of those required to sign.

One question on the sheet illustrated our confusion: "Will there be published a list of the 'parties and organizations' in which membership during the past five years is required to be listed by public employees?" *Answer:* "According to the best information we can get, probably not."

The most comprehensive statement by those opposed to the oath written during the predeadline October period was composed

38

by the San Francisco State College chapter of the American Association of University Professors.[5] The AAUP statement itemized the objectionable features of the new oath, declaring it unnecessary and ambiguous, a product of political hysteria that violated the constitutional provision against oaths other than the traditional positive oath. The oath was a political test; it undermined professional security and tenure, weakened the bargaining rights of public employees, was an attack on civil liberty and academic freedom, and would be the forerunner of further threats and repression. All these points were well-founded arguments against the oath, but the strength of the AAUP statement lay in the resolution urging repeal of the Levering Oath that was to be mailed to our legislators.

Marguerite and I smiled, however, when we thought of the likely response of Senator Jack Tenney and other "Red hunters" in Sacramento. "Give the name of everyone who signs that to the FBI" would not have been far off. We would know on November 2 how many faculty members would back the proud words of the AAUP statement with action.

It is by the goodness of God that in our country we have those three unspeakably precious things, freedom of speech, freedom of conscience, and the prudence never to practice either of them.

Mark Twain

Chapter 5

I TOLD WELL-MEANING RELATIVES that I was thinking about refusing to sign the new oath. The first to attempt to dissuade me from such rash action was my Aunt Marjory, who visited us in mid-October, accompanied by an artist friend. Aunt Marjory lived in Laguna Beach, a plush southern California beach town. She was the oldest exhibitor in the annual Laguna Beach Festival of the Arts, where works by local artists are displayed. The paintings in the festival are always nice, but a tourist spectacular every evening in which high school students and other townspeople pose as figures in masterworks has always seemed an abuse of the medium to me. The popular dramatization occurs only miles from Disneyland.

The friend who accompanied my aunt on her visit had made a fortune after the War Against Fascism by selling off at greatly inflated prices Orange County real estate that he had snapped up during the Great Depression. Both Aunt Marjory and her wealthy friend peeked behind the sofa in our Mission District flat as though they expected to find "Communist agents" hiding there. In our working-class neighborhood, the friend's Rolls-Royce sedan could not have been more conspicuous. As we talked, I glanced out the window occasionally, concerned that curious children might scratch the car. I tried to assure my Aunt Marjory that I knew what I was doing but I think she and her friend were not convinced that I wasn't really a dangerous Red. It was obvious her friend had come along only because my aunt had insisted.

Next, my brother-in-law stopped by one evening for a "man-to-man" talk. His family had fled Germany in the thirties, in the exodus of Jews lucky enough to escape Hitler's holocaust. His father had been a judge in the Munich courts. My brother-in-law's oldest brother had started an import business upon arrival in this country. After a short period in his original vocation as a brewmaster, my brother-in-law joined the import business.

He had read some political theory and, during the war, had served in the military government branch. He understood my predicament a little better than my aunt did, but my objection to that portion of the Levering Act permitting the state to draft all public workers as civil defense workers could not have meant much to him, since he had recently joined his neighborhood civil defense volunteers and met with them regularly to study "disaster manuals." I supposed they practiced with buckets and shovels for fire-fighting, wore CD armbands, and learned to tie bandages and perform mouth-to-mouth resuscitation. And the very first thing they did upon becoming Civil Defense volunteers must have been to sign the Levering Loyalty Oath!

The arguments propounded by the California Federation of Teachers made some sense to my brother-in-law, however. A CFT pamphlet explained, "The Levering Oath is in contradiction to the Federal Constitution since it imposes on public workers a political test for employment, deprives them of equal protection under the law as guaranteed in the 14th Amendment, and exposes them through its ambiguity to self-incrimination and perjury." Persuasive as the CFT arguments were, my brother-in-law thought it was more important for me to keep my job. As we walked to the door he grinned and asked, "How many of your friends in the California Federation of Teachers will refuse to sign?"

My father urged me to consider the issue carefully, and added that he would support whatever decision I reached.

On the evening of October 18, I tried to compose a statement. I changed my mind and tore it up, and then went for a walk. At about two o'clock in the morning, I made a firm decision. I had walked farther than I had thought, past Precita Park to the upper streets of Bernal Heights. I quickly retraced my steps, retyped my statement, and went to bed.

Next morning, I showed my statement to John Beecher when we met in the cafeteria and he thanked me for joining him. My next stop was the *Golden Gater* office, where I handed my statement to an assistant editor and told her to print it if she wished.

What follows is the full text of my statement:

I have determined not to sign the Levering Loyalty Oath after careful consideration of the principles involved even though recent faculty meetings convince me that the majority who might unite to form a bulwark against this vicious oath will knuckle under when the test comes. My reason for dissent is elementary. I'm loyal to the idea that freedom of speech, press and assembly are the inviolable rights of all men.

Constitutional guarantees of freedom of speech, press and assembly represent the fruition of the common effort by millions to make the world a happier place. I refuse to accept the tampering with these freedoms currently practiced by flag-waving superpatriots who argue that temporary suspension is necessary in the interest of national security.

I don't aspire to martyrdom. Those who might accuse me of this must understand that I have a personal stake in freedom. Art teachers are not expected to take stands on issues involving social change. This is the area of the sociologist, the historian, the economist, or the political scientist. Art is a world of sensation. Moral purposes and literary meanings positively hamper art. At least, this is what we are told. "Art for art's sake" is still the dominant philosophy that guides us.

The artist who believes that restriction of civil liberty has no effect on him needs only to look at the evidence of the past twenty years to see his error. Artists were the first to be condemned in Hitler's Germany. Every German artist of recognized stature today was forced to exhibit in the infamous Munich "Exposition of Degenerate Art" of 1937.

I defy anyone to show that I am anything except pro-Rembrandt and pro Homo sapiens. Finally, I state that I will not accept without protest the cowardly device of depriving me of my earned salary and my right to practice the profession for which I've trained myself. I will not conform! I intend to protest with every device at hand, political or otherwise, until the wrong done to the people of California by the Levering Loyalty Oath has been rectified.

I also addressed a copy of my statement to J. Paul Leonard, then president of the college. The campus newspaper published only excerpts but, after that, there was no way to back out.

I'm embarrassed when I read the statement today. Such patriotic language in our cynical world just won't do. It must have sounded very "uncool" to the administrators who read it. Now I wish I had left out the line about being pro-Rembrandt. That was almost like my own private oath. Still, it was about the way I felt.

Soon afterward, an Assistant Dean at San Francisco State who I had not met before called me to her office. I couldn't imagine what she wanted. She compared me with Candide, struggling with forces that I could not comprehend. She asked why I wanted to throw over a promising career, only to be used by people who hated our country. I assured her that I was over twenty-one, that I had already survived D-day, the defense of Bastogne, and other tests. It seemed that I would have only wasted my breath to try to explain the principle of academic freedom. As I left, I asked her to remember me as St. George. "Wish me good luck," I said, "I'm off to slay a dragon."

By the time I made the announcement that I would not sign the oath, everyone knew more about what had happened in the legislature prior to the adoption of the oath.[1] To prepare the legislature for his civil defense program in September 1950, Governor Warren had obtained bipartisan support by soliciting advice from the most powerful anti-Communist legislators. Senator Hugh Burns, an undertaker from Fresno, had by this date taken over the chairmanship of the state Senate's Fact-Finding Committee on Un-American Activities from Senator Jack Tenney. Burns was selected to introduce the governor's program in the senate. In the assembly, Julian Beck, chairman of the Subcommittee on Subversion and the Democratic floor leader, and of course Assemblyman Levering were given the job of carrying the governor's program.

Opposition in the Assembly to the Levering Act, once it was drafted and proposed, had been led by George D. Collins,

Jr., of San Francisco, and by Edward E. Elliott, of Los Angeles. Assemblyman Collins looked somewhat old-fashioned. Almost frail in physique, he wore high shoes and dark, vested suits. His voice almost quavered as he tried in vain to stop the stampede toward political conformity. He asked his fellow legislators to look at the real situation in California. They would find, he said, that the real power of the Communists in the Golden State was as a "flea on a dog's back." In the end, the only assemblymen to vote nay had been Assemblyman Collins, San Francisco; Robert L. Condon, Walnut Creek; Joe C. Lewis, Buttonwillow; and Edward E. Elliott and Lester A. McMillan, both of Los Angeles.

Tempers had flared in the Senate. Republican George Hatfield, an expert on parliamentary procedure, objected to the imposition of an oath on public employees that the senators, as constitutional officers, did not themselves have to sign. To counter this objection, Senator Tenney moved that the Secretary of State administer the oath to the senators after the Levering Oath was adopted. Tenney declared, "In this way, gentlemen of the Senate, no one can truthfully say that the Senate imposed an oath on any of the citizens of this state that the members of the Senate were not willing to take themselves."

Liberal Senator George Miller of Contra Costa county objected. He recalled that the disclaimer provision required disclosure of subversive associations within the past five years. He challenged Senator Tenney with the question, "What's the time limit?" Senator Tenney, in an obvious reference to what he considered Miller's past left-wing associations, replied, "Five years, you're safe!"

Miller rejoined angrily with a reference to Senator Tenney's own left associations when Tenney had been president of the Musicians Union in the early 1930s: "Put it back *twenty* years, and are you? I won't sign it unless you extend the time back twenty years!"[2] In the end, Senator Tenney's resolution was approved. Only Senators Miller and Hatfield refused to take the oath when it was administered by the Secretary of State, and when the senators voted on Senator Burns's bill containing the Levering Oath only Senator Miller cast a nay vote.

Chapter 6

ISCUSSIONS OF THE OATH were held throughout
October. One of the largest was a panel discussion
at the nearby Baptist Church (students and teachers
were never allowed to use campus facilities for their
meetings). Four faculty members and four students
representing a "balanced" variety of viewpoints made up
the panel.

Dr. J. Fenton McKenna, the dean who had okayed my
appointment, presented a moderate argument, saying that the
oath must be repealed by orderly, legislative methods. A teacher
held that the oath was an unpleasant fact of life and that we should
adjust to it. Herbert Bisno from the sociology department urged
noncompliance as the only acceptable strategy. For the moment,
he stopped just short of announcing his personal intention.

One of the student panelists read an interesting exposition on
the history of test oaths, starting with the Spanish Inquisition. She
told about the famous Christian martyr, Sir Thomas More, who
died rather than recognize King Henry VIII as head of an independent English church. Joan of Arc also died for refusing to deny her
beliefs. The student went on to tell about the Salem witch trials
and the oath that Hitler demanded of all German citizens. She
concluded what some had thought, at the beginning, might be
an academic lecture, with a cry for action, "Let's get rid of
the Levering Oath before our college loses a single teacher!"

After each panelist had presented a point of view, the

45

discussion was polite and somewhat detached. I had the feeling
that the Levering Oath had been imposed in another country,
at another time, and on another school.

One spark of excitement was struck when a student in the
audience suggested a strike. The moderates looked embarrassed,
stared at the table, and played with their pencils when the suggestion was applauded, and the discussion soon moved on to other
things. A student speaker banged on the table to emphasize his
point, "If there are Communists at San Francisco State they will
be the first to sign the oath!" As he spoke, I had mental pictures of
an English teacher slipping bits of theory of surplus value between
past and present participles and of a mathematics teacher drop-
ping a line about Marxist revisionism into a lecture on algebraic
equations.

I observed at that meeting, as I had at other discussions, that
the notion of the professor as conspirator was widely believed.
Small wonder, since it had been a mainstay of anti-Communist
propaganda for many years. It was also a favorite theme with
editorial writers of the 1950s who opposed the oath, but only as
a bad strategem in the eradication of "subversion." It never
seemed to occur to anyone that a Communist might oppose the
Levering Oath for the same reason that motivated non-Commu-
nists; that is, because the oath violated our rights of free
speech and assembly.

I was pleased to see the subversive professor notion
challenged by one of the students in the audience. She said that
we obviously gave students very little credit for intelligence.
A teacher who would use the classroom to promote a personal
bias would soon lose the respect and interest of students. She
continued with her challenge, saying that it was a stimulus to her
if a teacher held strong convictions about a subject. She saw no
danger to her education in the expression of personal convictions,
including unpopular political ideas, if they were identified as
the views of the teacher. She concluded by saying the Levering
Oath would make intellectual eunuchs of teachers. There was
some applause.

Another student interjected a point related to the concept

of the conspiratorial professor, which, to him, was an even more pernicious danger. He said that those who argued that Communists would be the first to sign had already accepted the basic premise of special oaths—that we can keep people from participating in society on the basis of their ideas. He had touched upon a concern of many, namely the psychology of test oaths.

The proponents of oaths requiring a denial of political beliefs suppose that the oaths separate the loyal from the disloyal. But if the excluded have deeply felt dissatisfactions and are not allowed to express them, how can the majority possibly learn what might remove the source of dissatisfaction? Without communication, any real danger to society could only be made worse.

Further, without doubt, the egos of the officials who demand special oaths are bolstered by the compliance of the signers. But does not the need to demand, under penalty of punishment, that everyone agree with their particular view of society, show a fundamental doubt in their minds? Could Assemblyman Levering, Senator Tenney, and Governor Warren really believe our institutions to be so shaky that their existence could be threatened by the presence of dissenters? An institution that everyone respects should stand on its own merit.[1]

Many of the people at the Baptist Church panel discussion knew that I had announced I would not sign the new oath, and a small group invited me to join them after the meeting for a glass of beer and more discussion. At the Market Street bar where we gathered, we returned to the strike idea. I said a strike would be impossible until the majority of students understood that the Levering Oath had nothing to do with loyalty.

I stated my opinion that the demagogues in Sacramento knew what they were about when they used the word loyalty to function as a smokescreen for the real issue. Then, as now, much misunderstanding resulted from the use of that word. One who sees the word and goes no deeper assumes that anyone who refuses to sign must be disloyal. If the Levering Oath and the oaths similar to it appearing all over the land like a fever had been called "statements of disclaimer," "affidavits of denial," or some equally cumbersome label, it is likely that the students of

1950 would *still* have accepted them with equanimity, though at least the negative connotation would have been apparent.

A slight, blonde young man who I had not seen before asked, "Is your position the same as the Jehovah's Witnesses?" "No, it isn't," I replied, "and that has been another real cause of misunderstanding. The Witnesses and other religious groups refuse to take *any* oath as a matter of principle, even the traditional Oath of Allegiance to the United States Constitution. They hold that their only allegiance is to God, and I respect their beliefs. But my objection to the Levering Oath is based upon the Bill of Rights and its guarantee of free speech."

As the month progressed, we held other meetings in our homes, at which we tried to bring people to our discussions who had not reached a decision. I remember particularly one meeting held in my family's Alabama Street flat.

A teacher said he was concerned because the oath required him to predict his future beliefs. He intended to sign but reason would compel him to write in a qualification in the space provided. The qualification would be that he would indeed advocate the overthrow of the government if conditions ever became so intolerable that the majority demanded it. He had made a note of what Abraham Lincoln had said on the same subject: "Whenever the people shall grow weary of the existing Government, they can exercise their *constitutional* right of amending it or their *revolutionary* right to dismember or overthrow it" (italics added).

A college administrator had told the worried teacher that the qualification might not be allowed as it would cause legal problems. It was suggested that a more prudent course would be to write a separate statement, but what he might do with such a statement was not made clear.

The intelligence of the man who told us of his plight had been insulted. When he tried to square reason with the requirement of the oath, he was told that the only safe course was to write in "no exceptions." We didn't hear from him again but certainly he was aware of his compromise. Thus weakened, it is unlikely that he spoke up again.

Chapter 7

THE STUDENT COMMITTEE FOR Academic Freedom organized many of the meetings that were held that October. One was at John Beecher's upstairs flat near Market and Castro streets. By then the deadline was only a week away, and several important matters were on the agenda.

Eighteen or so people from the San Francisco public schools and public agencies were present in addition to the State College teachers. We crowded into John's tiny Victorian flat where we nibbled crackers and sipped white wine. People were sitting on the floor of the crowded room.

Before we turned to the agenda, the conversation centered again on the effect of the oath. It was generally agreed that fear had silenced many persons. Colleagues who had been active in liberal causes didn't even want to discuss the issues. Others, without the slightest past interest in politics, had said they were determined never to become involved. Even so, my hopes were stirred by the apparent determination of the people at the meeting. Perhaps there would be more resistance than we had thought.

The first item on the agenda that evening was a report on recent conversations between the counsel for the American Civil Liberties Union and public workers contemplating defiance of the oath. The Northern California chapter had agreed to a court test of the constitutionality of the new oath. The plaintiffs would be representative of all groups—city workers, public school

49

teachers, college teachers, and so on. They would be selected as soon as it was clear exactly who the nonsigners were.

The Student Committee for Academic Freedom had organized a system of pledge-card donations in the hope that nonsigners could continue working without salary, as both a political gesture and a means of permitting classes to continue without interruption. The penalty provisions of the oath didn't state specifically that nonsigners would be dismissed. It merely said that they would be denied compensation, so there was some talk about continuing to work while we lived on savings and money contributed to the pledge-card fund. Some money had been collected, but certainly not enough to sustain everyone. It was agreed that the money would be made available on the basis of greatest need.

Further discussion of the possibility of working without pay led to the conclusion that we were being naive. The state wouldn't let a technicality stand in its way. What, then, would be the best course to follow after we were dismissed? Should we leave quietly or should we be ejected? If we decided upon a strategy of work without pay, we would probably be physically removed by the police. John Beecher argued that passive resistance would help people to understand the issue by dramatizing it and would also aid students who were trying to organize a strike.

However, Leonard Pockman, the physics professor, and three others, all of SCAF, vigorously opposed the idea. They believed that more students would be repelled by the sight of teachers being thrown into the street than would be attracted to our cause. Pockman and Beecher exchanged angry words. The city workers felt that passive resistance to dismissal would be ineffective in their case. It was clear there would be no unanimity on that point!

At the end of the evening, someone asked John to read one of his poems. His choice, one of his best, was very expressive of the fear that everyone felt:

> . . .and all this hue and cry
> over academic freedom
> will surely seem a tempest in a teapot
> a century or two from now

Of course it is a shame that Dr. Mitchell
                    had to go
He'd published many books
and was a credit to the faculty
                May you quote me?
                Oh no indeed!
I meant no criticism by my remark
It was a wise decision to dismiss him
                I just meant . . .
Really I didn't mean a thing
but Mitchell was my friend
Don't quote me though
I want that off the record[1]

The October events gave me ample opportunity to practice drawing and lettering. Several art students and I designed hand-bills and posters that we printed in off-campus shops. Some were printed at the Graphic Arts Workshop, the only artist group in San Francisco in 1950 to persist bravely in a political stance in the face of repression. The workshop was organized somewhat after the pattern of the famous Taller de Graficas Popular in Mexico. Irving Fromer, Emmy Lou Packard, Victor Arnautoff, Stan Koppel, Dick Correll, and other regulars printed a popular

calendar that showed the principal dates of labor history, made displays for Negro History Week, and designed a songbook for the folksongs of Malvina Reynolds. The workshop invited me to use their facilities on Valencia Street. One of my posters which was particularly graphic, I thought, depicted academie in chains. Another showed the Bill of Rights skewered on a bayonet.

By mid-October I had become sufficiently identified with the anti-oath movement and Left organizations such as the Graphic Arts Workshop to make our family the target of one of the ugliest signs of the time, the hate call. The first incident shocked us into an awareness of the social sickness as nothing else could have done. Marguerite answered the telephone.

I couldn't hear what was said because I was finishing up the supper dishes. Marguerite's face was ashen when she came into the kitchen.

"What's the matter?" I asked.

"You won't believe what I just heard," she replied and said the anonymous caller had demanded to know "why you God-damned Commies don't go back to Russia?" That was followed by a physical threat laced with foul words and curses.

We reported the incident to the police, but, so far as we knew, they did nothing. In the fifties, dirty, threatening phone calls to the homes of political heretics were common. After several such incidents, we ordered an unlisted number, which we still maintain.

The hatred of Communists expressed in obscene telephone calls reminded me of French journalist Claude Bourdet's reaction to life in the United States. In an article in *The Nation,* Bourdet observed, "Communists are so scarce, that practically nobody in the United States has ever met one; thus any amount of fear and horror can be aroused against them."[2]

Just six days after I announced that I would not sign, and coincidentally, on the same day that the Chinese "volunteers" poured across the North Korean border, I received a manila envelope by registered mail. The familiar "Department of Defense" return address was in the upper left corner. It contained orders to report for military duty on December 15! My naive

impulse to join the Reserve Army when I'd left the service
in 1946, something I had almost forgotten, had returned to
complicate my life in October 1950.

The next day, I met with my eleven o'clock class and then
hurried to a noon meeting at the Townsend Center on Haight
Street. The elderly pension advocates were a fearless group who
loaned their hall to the anti-oath students when the college
administration would not permit meetings on the campus.

My class had gone badly, contributing to my emotion as
I entered the hall. It was small and crowded — about three
hundred persons were there, according to the *Golden Gater*.
I had been invited to speak.

I stressed the irony of being under orders to serve in
the Korean War at the very moment that I was about to be fired by
San Francisco State College for sticking up for the Bill of Rights.
I asked, "How can I tell my fellow soldiers in Korea that they're
fighting for freedom when I know the Constitution is being
destroyed in California?"

"Just what *can* I tell them?" I demanded. "Shall I say that
democracy is safe in the United States when every newspaper is
filled with stories of people being blacklisted, careers being
destroyed, and people going to jail for nothing more than
nonconformity? Not really!"

The bitterness I felt put me in good form. The students
responded with loud applause and cheers. One of my friends in
the back of the room shouted, "Tell 'em, Frank!"

I continued, "Shall I say that people back home are guarding
the Bill of Rights while the soldiers fight and die in the freezing
mud of a strange land? Impossible! I'll have to tell them the truth,
that the rights of free speech, press, and assembly are being
mocked by our so-called leaders. I will say that our freedoms are
being turned into a shambles in the name of anti-Communism!"

I also told the students about the hatred that had been spewed
on my innocent family by anonymous telephone callers, and I
compared the flag-waving jingoisms of the war-mongers with
what was really happening to our freedoms. I also talked bravely
about student strikes and mass organizations, though secretly I

had resigned myself to the likelihood that not much would happen. October 1950 was not the time for radical militant action.

Lucy Hancock, who was a secretary in the education department, introduced herself after my speech at the Townsend Center. She asked if we could discuss the oath in more detail. We went to a restaurant on Market Street for coffee where we could talk. Lucy, at that time about thirty, was of medium height and stature and wore her brown hair in a neat, short cut. Her trim suit, her dark-rimmed glasses, and her alert, intelligent manner made her the picture of an efficient secretary.

I told her how I felt about the oath and my understanding of the penalty for defiance — that is, certain dismissal and possible blacklisting in the future. I urged her to talk with others before making her decision because we would certainly not be supported by the entire faculty or even a very large segment of it. In fact, supporters of our cause in general would be *few and far between*! I wouldn't want to think she had sacrificed her job because of my arguments alone. In spite of my suggestion for caution, however, Lucy made her decision as we walked back to the campus. She would not sign the oath!

By the last day of October we knew with some certainty who the nonsigners would be. Some faculty members, like Beecher and me, had made public statements. Others had confided their intentions to students or friends. Some who said they wouldn't sign actually did, but tried to rationalize their action with militant letters to editors, statements of protest, and news conferences. Some who had been most conspicuous at discussions in early October turned silent.

One of my advisors when I had been a student at San Francisco State was a professor of French, my minor department. He was an ascetic-looking young man whose principal passion, it seemed to me, was the works of Alfred de Musset. When he was approached with invitations to participate in demonstrations against the oath, he politely declined, and some time thereafter, left San Francisco State College. I learned later that he had applied for a passport from the United States of America and that this was granted, but only after intervention with federal authorities by the American Civil Liberties Union. I guessed that he had "belonged" to something, but what it was, I do not know.

There was a certain poignancy about the way the political heretics at San Francisco State became friends, an emotion not shared, I'm certain, by the college administration or the FBI agents who patrolled the campus. After reading her announcement in the *Golden Gater,* I sought out Phiz Mezey, the blithe, attractive journalism instructor and faculty advisor to the student newspaper. To explain how her decision came about, I must go back to the 1950 summer session.[3]

When Arthur Duffy, the feature editor of the summer-session newspaper received an *F* for his summer's work on the paper, he hinted that Phiz Mezey, the instructor, had "Communist" leanings. He claimed that Phiz gave him the failing grade because he had written editorials in support of the Korean War. In October, after the Levering Oath was enacted, Duffy renewed his attack on his teacher by taking his complaint to the San Francisco *Call-Bulletin,* a Hearst newspaper well known for its anti-Communist stance. Duffy's story was featured, since it went well with the *Call-Bulletin*'s constant barrage of antiradical editorials. Phiz saw the side-by-side placement of the Duffy anecdote with other loyalty oath stories as an obvious effort to malign faculty members, including the American Association of University Professors.

Phiz was quick to defend herself. "In the particular case cited," she protested, "the failing grade was given for defiance of the editor and insubordination and failure to cooperate with the newspaper staff. Mr. Duffy held the view that his page was his private property. The editor and faculty advisor rarely saw his copy before it was printed and staff editors were not permitted to edit it, although this was the established policy."

The *Call-Bulletin* continued to write about the alleged discrimination against Editor Duffy by his "left-wing" advisor. When the young journalism instructor went to one of the college deans for support, he advised Phiz to just "let things blow over."

But things didn't "blow over." Phiz was called to a meeting

of six members of the college administration and a Hearst reporter. She was given ten minutes to prepare a statement for the press, which she was to preface with a denial that she was or ever had been a Communist! Phiz stood up and faced the six men who made this ultimatum and said that she would not comply.

Phiz wrote a letter to State's then President J. Paul Leonard in which she made the following remarks:

I realize that the incident of giving a failing grade to a student is being used by the press at this time because of the loyalty oath issue. In view of what has happened, can I expect the Administration to be in a position to protect me? Can I or any other teacher in class or conference dare to voice an opinion or make a suggestion to a student? How should I, or other teachers, grade in the future? No failures for poor classroom performance? Should I look into the backgrounds, families and political viewpoints of my students before giving grades?

Her letter concluded with her decision: "I will not sign the loyalty oath now because I know that hereafter no teacher can adequately be protected under the law."

Student editor Arthur Duffy took a parting shot in the *Golden Gater:*

In any investigation there is only one person who can adequately represent me, and that is President Leonard, who knew about the matter long before the stories broke. I have faith in Dr. Leonard, who has opposed the anti-loyalty oath group, and is an avowed anti-Communist. Trust your faculty!

Charlotte Howard was a teacher at Frederick Burke School, an entity within the San Francisco State community that was a training center for college students seeking careers in elementary education. Frederick Burke was nationally renowned for its advanced, progressive program.

Charlotte was a petite, red-haired woman. I remember her more clearly as the understanding, kindly teacher of our three-year-old daughter than as a nonsigner of the loyalty oath. I would leave Nancy at Frederick Burke on my way to classes and Marguerite would call for her after work at the Emporium department store. I didn't learn that Charlotte was a nonsigner until some days after the deadline for signing had passed.

Herbert Bisno was an assistant professor of sociology and a popular speaker at student meetings. I remember him as an outgoing, friendly man with strong features and dark, wavy hair. He wore conservative grey suits and liked to twirl a watch and chain that he wore in his vest pocket. He was a very articulate speaker, and in the midst of a debate, would stroke his dark hair as he sought the precise word or phrase he needed for expressing his thought.

I recall a debate between Herb Bisno and a Mr. Van Pinney, a former Judge Advocate of the American Legion.[4] Mr. Van Pinney argued that the Levering Oath was a necessary measure and that persons who would not sign the oath deserved no consideration, they could find other jobs. Bisno countered that "to attempt to enforce loyalty indicated a lack of faith in the people as well as a misunderstanding of the nature of loyalty and would result in alienation rather than loyalty." The American Jewish Congress, which sponsored that debate, did not declare a winner, although the largely student audience showed their approval of Bisno's remarks by their applause.

In his statement announcing his refusal to sign the oath, Bisno said, "History will see that Salem witch-hunts took place in California in 1950, but that in spite of this, people of integrity who still believed in a democratic way of life rose up to the defense of the principles in which they believed."

Dr. Leonard Pockman, the professor who had made particularly urgent appeals for faculty unity in early October meetings, announced to his classes that he would not sign the oath. He and I became better acquainted when, sometime in October, we participated in the formation of an organization to work for repeal of the oath. Pockman came to my office one morning to tell me that an organizing meeting was to take place that evening in a downtown hall. College teachers, public school teachers, public workers, "screened" seamen, and all citizens interested in the oath had been invited. I told him I would like to attend and we drove downtown in his car.

The basement hall on McAllister Street was crowded. I was

introduced to the temporary chairman, a business agent for the Public Workers Union. The United Public Workers of America had been an early target of Red-baiters, having been attacked in New York City and Chicago as being dominated by Communists, and was expelled from the CIO in March 1950.

The featured speaker that evening was Vincent Hallinan, the vigorous Irish lawyer who had represented waterfront leader Harry Bridges in his deportation trial. I was very impressed by his speech. Hallinan cried out, "In these days everyone talks about *force and violence*. It seems to me that another phrase should get more attention. That phrase is *crime and corruption*!" And he gave his audience a little lesson in the law, citing felonies that are commonly prosecuted in every civilized nation—murder, rape, burglary, assault, and arson. People are justifiably detained and imprisoned if their guilt is proven for such antisocial acts.

But, Hallinan warned, we were dealing with a very different matter. The undefined advocacy of "force and violence" banned by the Levering Oath was not a crime. Advocacy, even of actions abhorrent to the majority, was protected by the constitutional guarantee of free speech. He concluded by stressing that ample laws on the books already protected us adequately from true criminality without the efforts of superpatriots in Sacramento.

After Hallinan's speech, people who had decided not to sign and some who were not decided stood up one by one to tell how the oath would affect them. When questions were asked, Hallinan and other organizers of the meeting gave the best answers they knew.

Toward the end of the evening an organization was formed to assist nonsigners in working for repeal of the oath. A long discussion ensued, frequently punctuated by laughter as puns were suggested for a suitable name. Joint Action Council for Repeal of the Levering Act was finally decided upon as the best description of our aim. The term *joint action* signified action by people from all walks of life. John Beecher was elected chairman and I was elected vice chairman. Ann Rosenfield, a social worker, was elected secretary, and Beb Bratt, draftswoman for the city, was elected treasurer.

Beecher accepted his office with an excellent speech. In my brief acceptance remarks, I assured everyone that I intended to be more than a mere name on a letterhead, that in fact I intended to devote every minute that I could find to my duties as vice chairman. I smiled at Leonard Pockman, who was seated next to me and remarked, "Well, it looks as though I've been duped." That was a term used in that fear-laden time to describe the entrapment of naive souls by Communist fronts. Pockman frowned at me. He was too much in earnest for my irony.

For this time lost, but not forever. We have learned. Tomorrow
the Cause will rise again, strong with wisdom and discipline.

Jack London
The Iron Heel, 1907

Chapter 8

ERTAINLY, I WOULD BE CALLED a dupe. I knew
that I would be told the Public Workers Union was
"dominated" at that time by Communists and that
Beecher and I had been recruited to obscure the real
leadership of the council. But so what? No crime had
been committed or was being contemplated. Wasn't the whole
experience a perfect example of the central evil of political test
oaths? Oaths divide people on the basis of irrational fear. To me,
the political beliefs of the meeting organizers were completely
irrelevant to our common opposition to the suppression of
free speech.

Before leaving me at my car, Leonard Pockman suggested
a drink, and we stopped at a place on Geary Boulevard. As we
sipped our drinks, we reflected on the meeting. Leonard
described the future as he saw it: "There will be a consolidation
of military and capital, with less and less civil liberty."

I asked, "How long do you think that situation will last?"

"It's hard to say," he replied. "It may last ten, fifteen,
twenty-five years, maybe longer. After all, in Europe it took the
War Against Fascism to end it." I said, "What you say reminds
me of one of my favorite stories, *The Iron Heel* by Jack London."

Then Leonard and I talked about our less political interests.
I talked about my favorite artists, especially Orozco and
Beckmann. He told about a book that he intended to finish in the
near future, designed to make mathematics a pleasure instead of

a trial for beginners. Before saying good night, we toasted the Joint Action Council for Repeal of the Levering Act with another round.

The list of nonsigners grew a little longer. The first person to announce defiance of the Levering Oath at San Francisco State had been John Beecher. I had been the second. Leonard Pockman, Lucy Hancock, Phiz Mezey, Charlotte Howard, and Herbert Bisno all announced their intentions before November 1.

The two remaining nonsigners at San Francisco State said nothing until the last moment. Dr. Eason Monroe, Chairman of the Division of Language Arts, and Jack Patten, an instructor in the English department, called a news conference late in the afternoon of November 2, only hours before the midnight deadline, to announce that they would not sign. That conference was well attended, since Dr. Monroe, in academic rank, held the most prestigious position of all the nonsigners.

Dr. Monroe spoke to the press in measured, carefully selected phrases. He was about forty years old, a doctor of education who had studied at Stanford. During the war, he had been an officer in the Navy, then he had taught at Pennsylvania State before coming to San Francisco State. His slim physique was complemented by a tweed suit and conservative necktie. His hair and brows were neatly trimmed. In the presence of Eason Monroe, I always felt that I should polish my use of the English language. The polite smile that accompanied his calm, reasoned remarks impressed the reporters.

His statement was right to the point: "The oath attacks the thing it purports to defend." He went on, "It may be that the lawmakers simply failed to understand the character of the American idea of loyalty; or it may be an effort, on the part of a small group of men, to distort the concept of earned allegiance, freely given, into one of sterile and forced submission."[1]

Jack Patten, the English instructor, said very little. He sat at Dr. Monroe's side and nodded in agreement as he chain-smoked.

As I left the campus on November 2, I picked up the latest *Golden Gater*. A front-page story carried comments by the nonsigners. John Beecher had told the reporter that he considered

61

it his duty under the Oath of Allegiance to fight the Levering Oath. Then I turned to the letters to the editor and found one critical of the lack of support for the football team. "How can we expect the team to go out and fight for us when the recognition they get plays second fiddle to a few malcontents on the faculty?" it complained.

Earlier in that day, San Francisco public school teachers, employees of the University of California, San Francisco municipal workers, and some of the State College teachers had been in court to seek a delay. The incident was described in the San Francisco *Examiner* for November 2:

As many workers struggled to get in under the wire, the new oath won its first Constitutional test in San Francisco court. Judge Molkenbuhr refused to stop public officials from firing or cutting off salaries of those who did not sign the oath. He commented, "The oath represents the legitimate exercise of the State's police power."

The attorneys for the heretical employees who went to court, Vincent Hallinan, Norman Leonard, and Benjamin Dreyfus for the public school teachers and municipal employees, and ACLU counsel Wayne Collins for the City College and San Francisco State teachers, failed to make a strong impression upon Judge Molkenbuhr in pleading for injunctive relief. Walter Peddicord, a San Francisco deputy district attorney, growled that the nonsigners should be fired, saying that the Levering Oath was a means by which California sought to preserve itself.

The November 2 midnight deadline for signing the loathsome oath passed!

At breakfast the next morning, Marguerite and I studied our *Chronicle* with intense interest.[2] The oath story had been buried in the newspaper by reports of other shocking events. On the previous day, Puerto Rican rebels had attempted to assassinate President Harry Truman right in the Capitol and a crackdown against New York's Puerto Rican community was under way. In Korea, General MacArthur's forces had not stopped the onslaught of Chinese infantrymen, who had stormed across the North Korean border on October 25.

Nevertheless, the oath story was reported and nonsigners

were listed according to their jobs. The breakdown of the fifty-one San Francisco nonsigners was as follows: eight teachers and one secretary at San Francisco State College; sixteen teachers in San Francisco public schools, including San Francisco City College; seven employees in the city child-care centers; one school department attendance bureau employee; two physicians on the Department of Education counseling and guidance staff; two Municipal Railway bus drivers; three social workers in the Public Welfare Department; an assistant probation officer at the Youth Guidance Center; three nurses at city or county hospitals; two draftspersons (both were women listed as "draftsmen"); one psychiatric social worker; one waiter in a municipal cafeteria; an engineer at the Third Street bridge; and a license clerk in the State Department of Motor Vehicles.

Marguerite reminded me that I still had classes to meet at the college. I put the newspaper aside and drove the Studebaker through the Mission district to Market Street, past the U.S. Mint, to a parking place near the college. I was still thinking about the list of nonsigners when I entered the drawing studio. I had no sooner hung up my hat before my students presented me with a card expressing their understanding of my defiance. I was very moved by their gesture and told them that I would continue to hold class until I was officially dismissed.

After class, several colleagues stopped me in the hall to tell me of the agony they had suffered. They agreed with me, they said, but just couldn't afford to lose their jobs. They assured me that their signing of the oath didn't mean that they would cease to work for its repeal. Curiously, all had hit upon a rationalization we were to hear many times—that they would be more effective against the oath if they worked against it from *within* the system.

On my way home, I bought several newspapers at the large newsstand on Mission Street. The Oakland *Tribune* of November 3 told of a teacher whose service dated back to the end of World War I. Her situation was particularly touching because she'd been about to retire: "When Miss Marguerite Ellis, 6100 Harwood Avenue, who refused to sign the oath, showed up as usual for her classes at Technical High School, she was met by Principal Will

W. Green, who handed her a letter informing her she had been relieved of her assignment." Because of the nature of her dismissal, Miss Ellis' stand would deprive her of all retirement benefits, which she had worked over thirty years to accrue.

There were more items about nonsigners in the East Bay. Two warehousemen at the Port of Oakland had refused to sign the oath. An Alameda County hospital worker resigned rather than submit. One teacher in a Berkeley public school and five teachers from Richmond were also listed as nonsigners in the *Tribune* story.

By November 3, 1950, the University of California had suffered from oath controversy for almost two years. At first, the issue was the special oath required by the regents; now the university was subjected to the new Levering Oath. Staunch opponents of the Regents' Oath had been fired or had accepted appointments at other universities, while many of the people who remained signed the Levering Oath, convinced that further resistance would be futile.

Russell Frazer was a teacher at UCLA who would later test the Levering Oath in court. He had signed the first oath required by the regents, but now refused to sign the Levering Oath.

Olaf Lundberg, then comptroller for the university, reported only seventeen dissident employees at the Berkeley campus. Officials at the other university campuses did not furnish statistics to the press immediately. Lundberg conceded that his figure was based upon early reports and promised a more complete report later, but a detailed report from the University of California was never released. In part, this lack may have resulted from the academic caste system, which virtually ignores non-contract staff below lecturer level in any statistic. The Joint Action Council for Repeal of the Levering Act, admittedly seeking a maximum figure, estimated that all nonsigners at all UC campuses, including full and part-time, teaching and nonteaching assignments, would total in the hundreds!

One teacher at Burlingame High School in San Mateo had refused to sign. A check of the Sacramento newspapers showed five nonsigners in the major state departments in the

64

capitol. Other counties reporting nonsigners were Shasta, Placer, Sonoma, Santa Clara, San Joaquin, Tulare, and of course, Los Angeles. (There may have been as many as 20 in the largest county in California.)

Clearly, more heretics were clustered in the San Francisco Bay Area than in other parts of the state, but this fact was not surprising. San Franciscans have always taken pride in their independent spirit. The city of Tom Mooney and the General Strike of 1934 might be expected to have a few residents who would spit on Assemblyman Levering's oath.

Also, proper credit for the strength of the San Francisco response is due to the people of our little council, who had worked hard in October to inform public workers about the oath. We had contemplated carrying our efforts to Southern California and rural areas, but we were prevented from doing so by a lack of time and money. In assessing the significance of the total number of nonsigners reported, we had to keep in mind that some people left their jobs without announcing the reason and so went uncounted, that the newspapers didn't mention the haste with which the Levering Oath had been passed by the state legislature, and that most public workers did not have enough information about it. But even so, my studies show that as many as 890 Californians may have refused to sign or resigned their jobs because of the oath. And there is no doubt that the figure for San Francisco, the principal locale of this book, was 51.

The newspapers even managed to get a little humor into their stories on the day of the big heresy count. It was reported from Los Angeles that a three-year-old had been hired to model for a junior college art class. She was told she would have to swear she didn't intend to overthrow the government by force and violence before she could be paid. As she couldn't read or write, her parents were told they could sign for her. They refused, but said she could pose for the art students without payment!

The November 3 evening San Francisco *Examiner* was dominated by a half-page drawing. Richard Nixon, who was conducting a smear campaign against liberal Helen Gahagan Douglas for a U.S. Senate seat, was shown in front of a stone

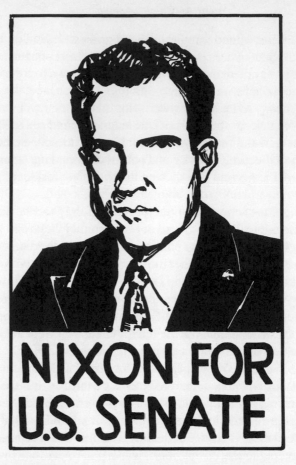

NIXON FOR U.S. SENATE

fence holding a shotgun in one hand and a dog-catcher's net in the other. Uncle Sam plowed a fertile field beyond the fence beneath a beaming sun. Scurrying away from Guardian Nixon were weasels, rats, and other assorted rodents labeled *Appeaser, Professional Pacifist, Spy, Conspirator, Soviet Sympathizer,* and *Propagandist*. Considering the hysteria of the time, it would have been difficult for the average reader not to have added another animal with the label *Loyalty Oath Nonsigner*.

Despite the gesture of confidence made by my class, and even despite the comradeship of Marguerite, I felt very much alone on November 3, 1950. The 890 Californians, out of a total population of 14 million, seemed very few and far between!

Now we waited for our dismissal notices. It would surely be just a day or two. I continued to meet my classes but instead of making assignments and conducting critiques, I simply drew from the model with the others and found, by chance, the very best way to teach drawing.

The college administration asked me to brief my replacement, who was already waiting to take over. I told them he could go to Hell, but then relented and put my lesson plans in his mailbox at a moment when I wouldn't have to meet him face to face.

Someone scrawled on our blackboard, "When the Scab walks in, we walk out!" That very distasteful label, even in the circumstances, seemed too much. I erased the blackboard and wrote, "Who can remember the name of the teacher who took Socrates' place?"

November 7, 1950, was Election Day. On the morning of November 8, the San Francisco newspapers ran a banner headline: "Warren, Nixon, Taft and Dewey in National GOP Triumph; Brown in Big Lead; No. 6 Crushed."

The headline referred to Earl Warren, who had defeated James Roosevelt to become reelected for a third term as Governor of California. The rewards of anti-Communist rhetoric had paid off. Richard Nixon had defeated Helen Gahagan Douglas in the U.S. Senate race. Nixon's campaign tactics would be remembered as classic smears. He had issued a pink sheet showing Mrs. Douglas's voting record to be similar to that of Congressman Vito Marcantonio, the radical politician from New York (Marcantonio was also defeated for reelection to the House of Representatives). This, even though Nixon had sometimes voted the same way as Marcantonio on aid to war-ravaged Europe.

Robert Taft had been reelected to the Senate in Ohio. Thomas Dewey would be New York's governor for another term. Californians had elected Edmund G. "Pat" Brown, the only Democrat named in the headline, to be their next attorney general. "Number 6" was a proposition which, if passed, would have legalized gambling in California.

I had a premonition, as I read the election returns, that this would be the day we would receive our dismissal notices. What a logical moment for the state college system to rid itself of its heretics! The irony was almost too good. I made a quick sketch before leaving for the college. And when I arrived, sure enough, there it was—a note on my desk instructing me to report immediately to the president's office.

Loyalty is a way of life, not an oath. It is a method, not a motto. Sound loyalty cannot be prescribed like a college course, it must be earned. Valid loyalty cannot be ordered around like a draftee on a parade ground, it must be desired . . . . if ever American loyalty becomes identified with blind allegiance to the status quo or with keeping our mouths shut, we are lost as individuals and as a nation.[3]

Edwin Broun Fred
Former president of the University of Wisconsin

Chapter 9

THE CLERKS IN THE OUTER ROOM of the president's office avoided looking me in the eye after I announced my name. They asked me to wait. I studied the cracks in the brown varnished anteroom wall, and after a few minutes I was handed a registered letter. I signed for it and went to my office to read it.

You are hereby notified that you are dismissed as an employee of the San Francisco State College effective November 8, 1950. The reason for your dismissal is as follows: You have been guilty of gross unprofessional conduct in that you have failed and refused to take and subscribe to the oath or affirmation within the time prescribed and as required of you by Chapter 8 of Division 4 of Title 1 of the Government Code of the State of California (Chapter 7, Statutes of 1950, Third Extraordinary Session).

The letter was signed by Roy E. Simpson, then State Director of Education.

I didn't expect the "gross unprofessional conduct" phrase. What could be more professional than to stand up for a principle, and especially for one involving an oath of disclaimer that almost every educated person agreed would be found unconstitutional?

The Student Committee for Academic Freedom, in street-corner rallies and in its November 8 newsletter, urged students to boycott classes, particularly those taught by "scabs." The college administration had, in fact, made public the names of our replacements immediately after the delivery of our dismissal letters. A few students did stay away on November 8, but the majority cited the need to complete degree requirements on schedule as their reason for not supporting the SCAF suggestion.

Meanwhile, an anonymous sheet called *The Prompter* had been widely distributed on campus in the days between the signing deadline and that of our dismissal. It claimed that SCAF was controlled by "Moscow agents," but that SCAF efforts to inspire a student strike, or more realistically, to organize a boycott of "scab" classes, had been hampered by *The Prompter*. However, apathy, fear, and misunderstanding of the new oath were already strong enough to guarantee our fate without the abusive efforts of the handout. There was no question now about our refusing to leave campus or to continue teaching without pay.

The attacks on the anti-oath students by its anonymous defenders received more attention than they deserved, and the waste of much time and energy resulted. Some students who were reluctant to act against the oath itself had a chance to salve their consciences by protesting the underhanded methods of *The Prompter*.

Dr. J. Paul Leonard, the college president, had reached his distinguished position after years of working upward on the academic ladder.[1] He received his BA from Drury College and his MA and PhD from Columbia. Then he taught at William and Mary College and at Stanford and had several published works to his credit.

Dr. Leonard's main concern in 1950 was the rapidly growing demand for a larger campus. The student body had grown from about 750 students at the beginning of his administration in 1945 to over 5,000 in 1950 and he anticipated that it might increase to 20,000 by 1980. It had not been easy to get the land and money that would be needed. In addition to thirty acres already purchased by the state, it would be necessary to purchase additional adjacent property from the Metropolitan Life Insurance Company, the City of San Francisco, and from Henry and Ellis Stoneson, the latter having planned a large residential and commercial development to the north of the existing site. Dr. Leonard explained the problem to his colleagues, "I had to get all

70

of the support I could in the Bay Area, then get funds to build an institution to serve 10,000 to 15,000 students. The money had to come from Sacramento, and I had to work with the state, to make them realize that we would have far more than 3,500 students, the maximum growth figure estimated by the state authorities."

Dr. Leonard said he didn't like the Levering Loyalty Oath any more than the next person, but beyond expressing his distaste for the law, there wasn't much else that he could do. In the mood I was in during November 1950, I thought he could have refused to sign it, just as I had.

Dr. Leonard was distressed to learn that Dr. Monroe and Dr. Pockman were among the nonsigners. Based upon their work together at Stanford, he had personally selected Monroe to head the Language Arts Division of the rapidly growing college, and he considered Pockman one of the very finest teachers at the school.

When he was asked what his attitude would be toward the nonsigners if the oath should ever be found unconstitutional, Dr. Leonard stated we had no rights to reinstatement based upon such an unlikely ruling:

Those who have not received tenure will be considered for reemployment, each on his own merit as a teacher, as would have been true before the oath was required, he replied. Court action alone will determine the future employment of those on tenure who have left us, and no amount of group action or pressure activities will influence this.

In the McCarthy era, more and more of Dr. Leonard's time would be diverted from planning for the new campus to soothing local politicians who attacked the college.

Joseph Alioto, then a member of the San Francisco Board of Education, charged that the college had "an atmosphere hostile to our basic political heritage."[2] Referring to the nonsigners, Alioto charged that the college has "the kind of atmosphere where a Marxist would be tolerated—as some have been."

Then Alioto added, "In my opinion the administration has been tolerant of Marxists in the past. Let them deny it. They may have fired those people when the loyalty issue arose. The question is why did they let them stay that long?"

Alioto was not certain how many Marxists might be on the college staff. Of the nonsigners of the oath he said, "I can't say they all were Marxists. Some might have conscientious objections — that's within their rights. But some of them — I'd say two or three — definitely were Marxists, in my opinion. This is based on what I discovered on my own. I don't want to name them at this time."

President Leonard responded to Mr. Alioto's charges, reaffirming that Marxists were not welcome at the college. "San Francisco State College does not tolerate Communists and the Administration believes it now has none on the faculty," he declared. He also invited local school board members to come to the college, to see for themselves if the college was a hotbed of radicalism. He said that if there was any doubt about the loyalty of any teacher at the college, "we ask a second study by the investigative staff of the State Department of Education."

To mark our dismissal, SCAF announced that it would hold a farewell rally on Monday morning, November 13, at 11:30 A.M.[3] Sound equipment and a flatbed truck were rented and a handbill urged all students to boycott classes. That rally was one of SCAF's most successful efforts. Even the conservative *San Francisco Chronicle* reported that one thousand persons jammed Buchanan Street in front of the college, but I'm certain the total was closer to two thousand. San Francisco police and the FBI patrolled the edges of the crowd while college administrators and their clerks peered warily from their office windows.

Highlights of the speeches still stand out in my memory. A SCAF spokesman, in an introductory speech, noted that San Francisco State College, under the Levering Oath, could not live up to Thomas Jefferson's ideal of what a free university should be. The student speaker quoted Jefferson: "This institution will be based upon the illimitable freedom of the human mind. For here we are not afraid to follow truth, wherever it may lead, nor to tolerate error so long as reason is left free to combat it."

Dr. Eason Monroe thanked the students for their efforts and urged them to continue supporting organizations that would work

72

for repeal of the oath.

As for Herb Bisno, he analyzed the impact of the oath upon the social sciences. By making free discussion of Communist theory difficult, the Levering Oath would negate the fundamental responsibility of social science to pursue, without fear or distortion, the search for knowledge and understanding. He also talked about the quasi-military status of teachers under the new oath. It would be difficult to predict what an unscrupulous political regime might impose upon the schools, he warned, with the powers granted by that section of the oath that made teachers subject to "such civilian defense activities as may be assigned to them by their superiors or by law."

Phiz Mezey stressed the equation of loyalty with conformity. Like most of the other speakers, she closed with a promise to return to the college when the oath was no longer required.

Leonard Pockman told the crowd that we were not alone, and he listed the heretics in other areas: public workers, state workers, and teachers in other schools who had refused to sign test oaths. He related our cause to the seamen who had been "screened" because of past or present political beliefs. He recalled how union leaders such as Maurice Travis and Hugh Bryson had defied the Taft-Hartley law, and spoke passionately for our brothers and sisters who had sacrificed careers in the arts. As he spoke, it was really not difficult to see, in one's mind, great masses of people marching against the oath.

John Beecher talked about the tradition of fighting bad laws and drew a parallel between the causes of Thomas Paine and other popular heroes of the American past with our own plight. According to Beecher, King George III undoubtedly considered the leaders of the American Revolution disloyal. Then Beecher turned from past history to the present, pointing out that the courts would not act in our favor unless public pressure was brought to bear.

Jack Patten said he had enjoyed his work at State and hoped students would remember our story. As I recall, Lucy Hancock and Charlotte Howard were the only nonsigners who did not appear at the farewell rally. Lucy was probably too busy with work at the office that had been rented by the anti-oath forces.

For a preface to my goodbye, I chose to read a quotation from Robert W. Hutchins, then President of the University of Chicago: "The question is not how many teachers have been fired, but how many think they might be, and for what reasons . . . . The entire teaching profession of the U.S. is now intimidated."[4]

Next, I made a prediction. I urged the students to remember to look back in ten or fifteen years to the current year, 1950. They would find, I believed, that 1950 was the year when meaningful choice in American politics came to an end. They would see that, from the time of the oath, they had merely legitimized the owners, call them Democrats, Republicans, whatever. The enemy among us, they would know, had been the unthinking politicians who had imposed the oath.

We climbed down from the flatbed truck to the cheers of most of the crowd and talked for a while with the students who remained. Newspaper reporters asked only a few questions. Someone showed me a letter in the *Golden Gater*. It contained these remarks:

Justice Robert H. Jackson at the Nuremburg War Trials said that the German people should have disobeyed the unjust laws! That, in the end it is the individual who must take the blame for his actions. Somehow I can't help but think that the firing of our teachers may be one of the most important incidents in our lifetime.

The voice of that student was heartening but I left the campus filled with somber thoughts, thinking that it would be a long, long time before I would return.

Chapter 10

THE RESPECTABLE ACADEMIC COMMUNITY was now behind us. All of our efforts had failed to save our jobs, to create a strike, or even to establish an effective boycott of classes! With good reason, students in the 1950s were called the "Silent Generation." Nor was it difficult to understand their silence.

By the end of our first week away from the campus, the little office rented by the Joint Action Council for Repeal of the Levering Act became the hub of anti-oath activity. At least now I would be able to devote some time to my duties as vice chairman since I had been granted a six-month deferment of my military service, originally set to begin on December 15. To help us financially, a supporter of our cause, who had invented a wheel-balancing machine, gave me a part-time job in the shipping department of his Emeryville machine shop.

The Joint Action Council office was on the second floor of a wedge-shaped building at the intersection of Market and Turk streets. We could see the Golden Gate Theater from our window and a credit dentist was next door. A pudgy man with a permanent grin operated the combination freight and passenger elevator. As we rode up or down, he would ask such questions as, "How goes the revolution?" He probably kept notes on our visitors. The building seemed stale, hostile, and had a sour atmosphere of futility, especially after I learned that other heretical organizations promoting other unpopular causes had preceded us at the same address.

Ann Rosenfield was our secretary. Marguerite and I had known her since 1947, when her husband, Allan, and I were in the Waterfront Chapter of the American Veterans Committee. The AVC organizers had hoped that the committee would be a liberal alternative to the American Legion for returning veterans of the War Against Fascism, but like a lot of liberal organizations of the period, it was virtually driven out of existence by the Red-baiters.

When we first met, I was a warehouseman and Allan was welfare director for the San Francisco CIO Labor Council. Ann spoke with a slight drawl that reminded me of Lauren Bacall, and her beautiful blonde hair made the resemblance more striking. Her first husband had been in the Army Air Corps in the War Against Fascism and had been killed in action. Ann had been a case worker in the San Francisco Welfare Department BTO (Before the Oath).

In the early fifties, a San Francisco radio commentator, Jimmy Tarantino, patterned his exposures of "subversives" after the staccato style of Walter Winchell. One evening, he linked our Joint Action Council to the "Communist conspiracy." It seemed obvious that one of our volunteers had supplied Tarantino with his material.

Ann's response to my excited telephone call to inform her of this attack was made with the same calm she showed in every crisis. "Oh yeah? What else is new?" Then she changed the subject to a much more important matter to her—how could we locate a few volunteers to lick envelopes for a big hand-bill mailing?

The handbill was designed to publicize a rally at which Carey McWilliams would be the principal speaker. His new book, *Witch Hunt,* described the inquisition we were experiencing precisely.[1] McWilliams was well known in California as a lawyer and as head of California's Division of Housing and Immigration, as well as the author of *Factories in the Field* (Archon Books, 1939) and *Brothers Under the Skin* (Little, Brown, 1942). With McWilliams as our speaker, we would certainly draw a good crowd, I was certain.

76

The rally was at the old Scottish Rite auditorium on Van Ness Avenue. I decorated the speakers platform with a banner that stretched from one side of the hall to the other. With bold red letters, I painted Thomas Jefferson's words, "I have sworn upon the altar of God eternal hostility against every form of tyranny over the mind of man."

John Beecher was the master of ceremonies and Jim Wood sang some rousing folk songs. Marguerite Ellis, who had been dismissed from the Oakland schools where she had taught since 1919, made a brief but impressive speech. No, she didn't regret her action! She quoted a passage from Mark Twain's *A Connecticut Yankee in King Arthur's Court:*

Under that gospel, the citizen who thinks he sees that the commonwealth's political clothes are worn out, and yet holds his peace and does not agitate for a new suit, is disloyal; he is a traitor. That he may be the only one who thinks he sees this decay, does not excuse him; it is his duty to agitate anyway, and it is the duty of others to vote him down if they do not see the matter as he does.

Miss Ellis was followed by State Senator George Miller from Contra Costa County. Throughout the fear-ridden 1950s, he was the only state senator who consistently opposed the oath, and in his speech he promised to work for its repeal.

Eddie Tangen, a Communist leader of the Marine Cooks and Stewards Union, told about the "screening" of seamen on San Francisco's waterfront.[2] Next, I was called upon as another warm-up speaker, and I tried to explain the effect of repressive oaths upon the arts.

Then Carey McWilliams made a brilliant and incisive analysis of the oath. "Test oaths are not in any way concerned with security, but with conformity," he declared. "They are specifically barred by the Constitution and undermine the meaning of American citizenship. And when you destroy that, you destroy the meaning of America." He described the fear of unseen bogeymen and fear of ourselves—senseless, irrational fears—that were being created in every part of our society. "The people behind the conformity program have one common characteristic. They cannot reason. They are massive in their imposition of their will on the people of the United States," he declared.

There were other meetings. Some were well-attended, but not many new supporters appeared. In fact, the first months of 1951 found the heretics talking more and more to each other, and, even worse, the anti-oath people occasionally succumbed to the all-pervading fear of the time.

As interest lagged, the anti-oath efforts were assumed by a new "organization of organizations," the Federation for Repeal of the Levering Act. An office was rented at 435 Duboce Avenue, and Dr. Eason Monroe, the former San Francisco State professor, became the federation's chairman. Lucy Hancock, the nonsigner from State's education department, became the secretary. Both were paid very small salaries. A few of the affiliated organizations were the Academic Assembly, University of California, Berkeley; the American Association of Psychiatric Social Workers, Northern California; the American Association of University Professors, San Francisco State College; and the American Federation of Teachers, Local 61. In general, the federation was composed of liberal and educated people, those who promised to resist "from within the system." The Joint Action Council continued its work, but its efforts at working with the new organization were not always welcomed.

The Joint Action Council had already sponsored a rally at the Scottish Rite auditorium, but since the council had been branded a "Communist front," the federation booked the same hall at a later date for a program designed to motivate the liberal community. The plan had been to stage a debate between Carey McWilliams on one side and Senator Tenney and Assemblyman Levering on the other, but the composer of "Mexicali Rose" and the author of the oath declined to participate. McWilliams was disappointed, remarking that he had looked forward to a debate with Tenney and Levering. Carey McWilliams continued to hit hard at the witch-hunters without fear of guilt by association.

Perhaps the most ambitious project attempted by the Federation for Repeal of the Levering Act was a statewide conference of opponents of the oath. The conference was held in a

Fresno hotel, a location that was easier for people in Southern California to reach than San Francisco, the federation's home base. John Beecher, Ann Rosenfield, and I attended the conference as representatives of the Joint Action Council. A few good resolutions came out of the conference, but the real purpose was forgotten because of a wrangle with the legislative representative of the Congress of Industrial Organizations (CIO), Mr. John Despol, who, it was alleged, had worked closely with Senator Tenney's committee and who insisted we would have to police our own ranks if we hoped to have his support.

The federation often consulted with the staff of the American Civil Liberties Union, Northern California. While the Northern California branch of the union was largely autonomous, it must have been painfully aware of a resolution that had been the cause of a bitter dispute in the ACLU since 1940. In *The Noblest Cry; A History of the American Civil Liberties Union,* Charles Lam Markmann stated, "Even the Union was not immune from the national purge fever: on February 5, 1940, years of resentment of the presence of fellow-travelers in its directorate and National Committee culminated in a narrowly won resolution by the board to bar from office or employment in the American Civil Liberties Union all adherents of any kind of totalitarianism; this was followed by the bitterly contested ouster of the lone Communist director, Elizabeth Gurley Flynn, when she refused to resign." Elsewhere in his study, Markmann remarked upon the ACLU's view of the Communist Party: "The Communist Party in the United States, the Union says, has a dual character: it is at once a domestic political entity and the instrument of an international conspiracy directed from a foreign headquarters."

Many thoughtful friends and leaders of the American Civil Liberties Union, including the vice chairman of the Northern California branch, Dr. Alexander Meiklejohn, were dismayed by the union's apparent inconsistency.[3] But controversies within the ACLU did not seem to affect me and other nonsigners at San Francisco State, or at least so I thought.

I went to the ACLU's old lower Market Street office sometime in October 1950, hoping to learn if any options were open to me if my deferment from military service could not be extended. I had already tried to resign my commission, but when the government refused my resignation, I thought that perhaps the ACLU could advise me of what my status would be if I took more drastic steps.

After some discussion of my questions, Mr. Ernest Besig, the hard-working executive director, changed the subject. From behind his desk, piled high with pleas from little people who had run afoul of loyalty laws, he told me that the ACLU Board of Directors had learned that John Beecher and I were officers in a "united front" called the Joint Action Council for Repeal of the Levering Act. He went on to say that it would be difficult for the union to support us if we continued in that association. (I believe my name had already been submitted to the union's general counsel as a potential plaintiff in a lawsuit to test the constitutionality of the Levering Act.) Somehow, what Mr. Besig had just told me didn't seem right, even with my knowledge of the controversial 1940 resolution of the national ACLU directorate.[4] That action had applied only to board members and employees of the union. I had not thought until that moment that the American Civil Liberties Union made a test of one's associations a prerequisite for its services.

The ACLU's general counsel in Northern California was Mr. Wayne Collins, a small, wiry, grey-haired man. One felt that the leather chair in front of a wall lined solidly with handsome law books was his natural place in the world. His stern manner softened when he reminisced about his defense of Japanese-Americans who had been held at Manzanar, Tule Lake, and other wartime concentration camps, or, in what seemed to me an extreme test of his dedication to civil liberty (coming so soon after the War Against Fascism), his spirited championing of "Tokyo Rose," the young American woman from Los Angeles who had broadcast propaganda from Tokyo. Collins had led a team of defense attorneys at her trial for treason.

A group of teachers who had refused to sign the oath gathered in Mr. Collins' eleventh-floor Mills Tower office to discuss the strategy for testing the constitutionality of the

Levering Oath. In the group were five teachers who had been
at San Francisco State, including myself; one teacher from
San Francisco City College; and one teacher who had worked in
the San Francisco high schools. Mr. Besig, the ACLU executive
director, was also there. Collins' opening question was a shock:
"How many of you gentlemen are members of the Communist
Party?"

I was the first to reply. I said, "I wouldn't know one if he
was seated right next to me." Even though I hadn't really meant
my remark as a joke, the others laughed, somewhat nervously
I thought, but at least the tension had been broken.

Some of the teachers were angry. When they protested that
the question mocked the principle that had brought us together,
Collins replied that he had to know *everything* about us. He
demanded that we respond to the question but conceded that each
person could answer privately. The discussion of the lawsuit
continued at length, almost a monologue on the law by the ACLU
counsel. As he went on, I pondered the propriety of his question.

When details of the proposed lawsuit were released to
the press, Mr. Collins volunteered the information that none of
the petitioners was a Communist. (One person at the Mills Tower
meeting revealed later that he had resigned from the Communist
Party at about that time.) It had been decided that the petitioners
would be two representatives from the state college level, one
representative of the junior college system, and one who had
taught in the high schools. Collins selected them, he said, because
of their tenure or because of other aspects of their personal
histories that would strengthen the case. *Pockman* v. *Leonard,* as
the case is called in legal records, was to go to the First Appellate
Division of the District Court of Appeal.

John Beecher and I dismissed Mr. Collins as our attorney
after the meeting in the ACLU counsel's office. At the moment of
Mr. Collins' question about our political affiliation, I had
assumed that, like any competent attorney, he simply had to have
all the facts and that nothing more should be inferred from his
question. But John saw things more clearly and, as always, was
uncompromising. He insisted that there was clear evidence that

the American Civil Liberties Union had yielded principle in the face of the anti-Communist hysteria. Mr. Collins' question only reinforced his conviction

Actually, our decision to dismiss Mr. Collins had already been rendered moot except as an expression of principle. The Board of Directors had empowered a Subcommittee on Academic Freedom made up of Messrs. Meiklejohn, Caldwell, Barrett, and Besig to determine if ACLU support should be withdrawn from John Beecher and Frank Rowe.[5] The *Board Minutes* for November 2, 1950 announced their decision:

Item 8—The Committee considered the problem presented by two nonsigners of the State oath who have sought our support, and who have since become Chairman and Vice-Chairman respectively of a united front known as the Joint Action Council for Repeal of the Levering Act. A motion was adopted to withdraw the Union's support from such persons if they continued with their support of the particular united front.

Before leaving the college, I had been told by a dean that, like Voltaire's Candide, I would encounter disaster wherever I went in our less than perfect world, and I had replied that I would prefer to be compared to St. George. Now, as John and I rode off to find another attorney, I felt more like Don Quixote's faithful Sancho Panza.

Benjamin Dreyfus, a veteran San Francisco civil rights attorney, agreed to consult with us without questions about our associations.

While we continued with our efforts, the frustration of the Korean War went on. Two hundred thousand American and South Korean troops were evacuated from North Korea in what General MacArthur's press officers called "an amphibious landing in reverse."

Also at that time, Joseph McCarthy was approaching the peak of his shameful career. From February 1950, when he had attracted nationwide attention with his charge that he knew of 205 Communists in the State Department, McCarthy lunged on with his below-the-belt, unfounded, and bullying charges until his name became synonymous with the era.

The result was to be expected. We read that, in a test
of popular attitudes, students had been handed copies of the
Declaration of Independence without identification. When asked
to sign a petition supporting its principles, they refused. They
said it was too "subversive."

It's hard to believe now that we had the temerity in late 1950
and early 1951 to take our story to the people on the streets. Yet
we kept marching. I remember going to Oakland to demonstrate
in front of Technical High School, where Marguerite Ellis had
been a teacher. The Joint Action Council had hoped to stimulate
interest in her appeal against her dismissal which might move the
Oakland Board of Education to reconsider. Only one other person

joined me in response to the Council's call for marchers.

Technical High School stretches along two blocks of Oakland's busy outer Broadway Street. The surrounding neighborhood in 1951 was lower middle class, with signs of tarnish. The Chamber of Commerce called Oakland the "All-American City." As the two of us demonstrating there walked back and forth with our signs, many people stared from their cars and not a few yelled "dirty Commies" or similar epithets. Someone threw a Coke bottle which I nimbly dodged.

Those of us who continued to work against the oath soon learned to recognize the FBI and Army Intelligence agents who attended all our meetings. They also harassed us in our homes. In one incident, two men with skinny neckties, grey suits, and grey eyes knocked on the door of my family's Alabama Street flat. I guessed who they were before they identified themselves. When one held out his opened wallet, I glanced at his FBI card and said nothing.

When the agent asked, "Frank Rowe?" I nodded. "We

84

would like to talk with you. May we come in?" "No, we can talk here, on the porch, if there's anything to talk about," I told him. He didn't like that but agreed.

They wanted to know about my friends in the Joint Action Council and the Graphic Arts Workshop but I cut them off. "If you have information that anyone I know has committed a crime, please tell me," I said. "Otherwise, you'll have to excuse me, because I have work to do."

The FBI agents left when they understood I wouldn't co-operate, to watch our house for about an hour from their unmarked Ford sedan.

One day I encountered one of my former drawing students while walking on Market Street. She showed me a recent copy of the *Golden Gater*. It seemed that the oath had been forgotten. The front-page story informed the college community that movie stars June Allyson, Dick Powell, and Rhonda Fleming were to visit State. I flipped through the rest of the newspaper. Not a word about academic freedom or the oath. But it wasn't just that those issues had been forgotten; it was fear. It was the fear we had seen divide the very people who opposed the oath, the fear that had caused even the most prestigious civil libertarians to flinch under fire, the fear that had kept our friends from marching. We would have to wait and see what developed in the courts.

Chapter 11

I N APRIL 1951, the Third District Court of Appeal ruled that the University of California Regents' Oath was unconstitutional! Some of the plaintiffs in the action, called *Tolman* v. *Underhill,* had taken other positions far from the Bay Area. Two, including Edward C. Tolman, professor of psychology, were at the University of Chicago, three were at Harvard, one at Carnegie Tech, one at Tulane University, one was working on a Rockefeller grant at UCLA, and one was at the Institute for Advanced Study at Princeton.[1]

Initially, there was rejoicing among the heretics when the news was announced. The attorney for the protesting professors, Stanley A. Weigel, expressed "gratification." In the long run, he said, the decision may well mark the turn of the tide against a "dangerous and un-American trend to judge men by what they sign instead of by what they are." Even though the Levering Oath was required of all university employees by this date, the Tolman decision seemed to indicate that the turning point in the struggle against repressive oaths had been reached.

Nonsigners of the Levering Oath who had been discharged by public schools, the state colleges, and other public agencies took heart. Surely the victory at the University of California would serve as a precedent for a ruling on *Pockman* v. *Leonard,* the Levering Oath case. In rapid order, three more suits were activated, *Frazer* v. *Regents, Bowen* v. *County of Los Angeles,*

86

and *Hirschman* v. *County of Los Angeles*. But the rejoicing aroused by the April 1951 decision was short-lived. The University of California Regents decided to appeal the ruling against their oath. This meant that by June 1 five cases involving loyalty oaths were pending in California courts, the appealed ruling and four others. On that date, the California Supreme Court announced that it would take up all pending loyalty-oath cases "as a matter of great public importance."

Upon hearing this news, Ann Rosenfield and I went back to our little upstairs council headquarters on Market Street, the sinister "front" that I had been warned against, to crank out more leaflets, mail more letters, and appeal for support from our legislators.

Dr. Eason Monroe, Herb Bisno, and Mort Elkins, the non-signing high school teacher, tried to register as lobbyists for the Federation for Repeal of the Levering Act. This was not allowed, even though lobbying through registered representatives has always been an established procedure. Senator Hugh M. Burns, the undertaker from Fresno and chairman of the state's un-American committee, disparaged their application, saying that any teacher who refused to take a loyalty oath was not entitled to appear before legislative committees.[2] Dr. Monroe told me later that, at one point in that dismal proceeding, a member of the committee had implied that Eason ought to go back where he came from. In anti-Communist idiom stemming all the way from 1917, "back where you came from" has always been assumed to mean Russia. With a wry smile, I'm certain, Dr. Monroe informed his inquisitor that he'd been born in the small California Sierra town of *Loyalton*.

On one of our visits to the Capitol to talk with politicians, we became acquainted with a nonsigner, Glenn Carrico, who had been an employee of the California Department of Employment. Mr. Carrico met us in the lobby of the Senator Hotel, then went with us as we buttonholed the assemblymen and senators. Afterward, we drove to his small farm several miles from the city where he, his wife, and three sons had milk cows, chickens, rabbits, and a garden. He planned to sustain his family with

87

the food he raised and money from milk sales until he found another job.

We stayed overnight at the Carricos' farm. Mort Elkins was with us. Mort had been raised in the city, so his admiration for the resourcefulness of the Carricos amused everyone. In spite of his problems, Glenn invited us to stay at his farm whenever we were in Sacramento.

It seemed to me that the loss of financial security had hurt Glenn less than the feeling that his work with the state had gone unappreciated. He felt isolated in Sacramento, where he didn't have the moral support of other nonsigners. And he told us how his children had been ostracized by their classmates because of his stand. The father of one child spread the word that he considered the Carricos "Commies" or "Pinkos." Other neighbors who could see what was happening would not raise a finger to help.

Even though we sensed Glenn's pessimism, we evidently did not realize the intensity of his feeling. Everyone in the anti-oath movement was shocked to learn, sometime later, that Glenn Carrico had walked into his bedroom and killed himself with his rifle.

After his suicide, Mrs. Carrico and her sons tried to carry Glenn's arguments for repeal of the Levering Oath to the public. When I asked Mrs. Carrico about Glenn's tragic death, she told me, "My children passed out the leaflets and I distributed them at the state buildings in the early morning hours before going to work. As a direct result, I am sure, I was soon dismissed from my job at the Roseville Community Hospital. Another person was also dismissed and we surmised that it was because I had hired her."

Glenn's son William recalls making several speeches about the oath in his eighth-grade classroom. The teacher eventually asked William to drop the subject, since it was embarrassing for him and he risked losing his job if he agreed with young Carrico's position.

When I told another son, James, that I was writing this book, he wrote to me, "I hope that they [Glenn Carrico's grandchildren] understand that Glenn Carrico was a man so passionately patriotic and devoted to the principles of his country's democracy that he could not bear living in it if there was going to be tyranny or deceit for our nation's future."[3]

In the backwash of these real and tragic events, painters and poets continued to express themselves. I tried to keep up with what they were doing when I could spare time from political activities. I found that most poets and painters, starting almost at the same date as the first loyalty purges, had moved toward obscurantism in their work. Oriental mysticism became the inspiration for many. Years of probing into private lives, screening, blacklisting, and loyalty probes helped to bring abstract expressionism to its zenith. Jackson Pollock, who had learned his craft from crusty old Thomas Hart Benton and had been influenced by Orozco, perhaps the most expressive of the Mexican muralists, retreated from reality while dripping gallons of paint onto sometimes startlingly handsome canvases. He ended it all by driving drunk into a tree. Pollock became the most publicized painter of the decade. Ezra Pound, who had propagandized for the Fascists, was restored to grace.[4]

Seymour Locks, who had recommended me for my job at State, and other artist friends became leaders of the abstract expressionist movement in San Francisco. A kind of mystique grew up around the California School of Fine Arts on Chestnut Street. Clifford Still and Mark Rothko led a movement away from the social commitment many artists had felt until then. Their students—Richard Diebenkorn, David Park, Hassel Smith, and others—painted huge unsized canvases with loosely brushed abstractions. The sculptors formed their work from the junk and nondescript throw-aways of consumer society to express, sometimes with indisputable power, the alienation that characterized their lives.

I believe it is not too farfetched to say that abstract expressionism was the aesthetics of the McCarthy period. Every abstract expressionist painter and sculptor lived in a private dreamland, where suicides, smashed careers, and purposeless existence couldn't reach them. This was an irony indeed, if my theory is true, because many reactionary know-nothing politi-

cians tried to make a few points by attacking the artists as
alien and subversive influences.

At that moment, my feelings about art were very split.
I experimented with avant-garde ideas. I was attracted by
San Francisco's North Beach, which had become the spiritual
home of the Beatniks, a few with real genius but most only
alienated from the trials of industrial civilization and the hysteria
of anti-Communism. The Beatniks lost themselves in North
Beach bars and tenements with abstract art and poetry, booze,
dope, Zen, and sex. I displayed a few of my pictures in a bar
where poets read their work, but my identification with that
part of San Francisco was very slight.

I was heartened to learn that other artists had refused to sign
the oath. Robert McChesney, the well-known painter, was one.
He taught both at the California School of Fine Arts and in the
San Francisco public schools in 1950. Others were Ed Cerney,
who had been at Stockton College, Eugene Bielawski, formerly
at Samuel Gompers Trade School, and venerable Coit Tower
muralist Bernard Zakheim, who was living in Sonoma County.

I visited occasionally with the artists at the California Labor
School and continued to work at the Graphic Arts Workshop.
Through Giacomo Patri, the school's art chairman, I met Anton
Refregier, one of the rare artists who had stuck by his political
conscience. Refregier had just completed his Rincon Annex Post
Office murals assisted by Louise Gilbert and Pele DeLapp,
members of the workshop. The murals were threatened by
reactionary politicians because Refregier had dared to depict
San Francisco's true history. Congressman Hubert Scudder from
Sonoma said, "These murals are an insult to the public and
anti-American in motif."[5] Scudder was particularly incensed
because Refregier had depicted the General Strike of 1934 in one
panel and in another had painted the Soviet flag among the flags
of other nations at the 1946 United Nations charter signing in
San Francisco. A panel in which a portrait of FDR was planned
had actually been cancelled due to protests by reactionary
Republican members of Congress.

Since the loyalty probers in the 1951 session of the

legislature were preparing new thought-control laws, however, I had precious little time for any kind of painting. Posters and leaflets were needed more than ever.

Senator Tenney let fly a barrage of bills—one for the removal of any public school employee "for the utterance of any treasonable or seditious words," and another to require the Levering Oath of all candidates for public office. Still another of Tenney's bills would have given employers complete discretion to fire or refuse to hire persons who were members of "organizations that advocate overthrow of the government by force or any illegal or unconstitutional means."

Senator Burns introduced bills to require the Levering Oath of lawyers and of businesses requesting licenses or permits of the state. Assemblyman Chapel introduced a bill to authorize wiretapping. Assemblyman Luckel jumped into the act with a bill to prohibit the use of school property to "members of organizations who advocate, or commit acts intended to further any program or movement the purpose of which is to accomplish the overthrow of the government of the U.S. by force, violence, or other unlawful means." Senator Dilworth introduced a bill to give the State Department of Education authority to investigate teachers and the right to require a specific denial of Communist Party membership.

The only proposals to become law out of all of this hysterical bilge were the Luckel and Dilworth Acts, but the defenders of the Bill of Rights certainly had their work cut out. Since Assemblyman Levering's name was on the oath that gave substance to all the others, it would seem that he had decided to save his energy for another big one.

That big one was not long in coming. Assembly Constitutional Amendment Number 9, by Levering, and Senate Constitutional Amendment Number 1, by Tenney, proposed simultaneously, would make the Levering Oath a permanent part of the state constitution. The Joint Action Council and the Federation for Repeal of the Levering Act mustered all of their forces when this legislation was introduced. Mailings, press releases, rallies, posters, and car pools to Sacramento had

91

to be organized in an effort to defeat the bills.

The hearing room in which the constitutional amendment was to be debated crackled with hostility.[6] Assemblymen looked at the citizens who had car-pooled from the Bay Area as though they were revolutionaries straight from the Kremlin. The people glared back. After Assemblyman Levering had spoken at some length, chairman Ernest Crowley asked, "Does anyone wish to speak against the proposed amendment?"

Dr. Monroe, for the Federation for Repeal of the Levering Act, and Joseph Landisman, for the Lawyer's Guild, asked to be recognized. Assemblyman Randal F. Dickey demanded that both men first say if they were Communists. When they politely refused, Dickey moved to deny them the right to speak because they were not registered as lobbyists. The Dickey motion passed.

My friend Seymour Locks asked permission to speak. He was a good person, who supported the federation in every way he could, but he was very conscience stricken because he had signed the oath. A member of the committee asked him if he had signed it. He replied in the affirmative, but I could see that for him to have to say it to the bully left Seymour crushed. But he stuck it out and managed a short but impressive defense of his former colleagues at the college.

Next, John Beecher identified himself and requested permission to speak. He added that he was not appearing for any group but would speak as a private citizen. After a whispered conference among the assemblymen, Chairman Crowley instructed Beecher to be brief.

John and Harold Levering were not more than three feet from each other. There sat the author of the oath, the instrument that had destroyed our careers, face to face with the man who, as much as any other person, symbolized our resistance.

Assemblyman Levering, I would have guessed, was about fifty-five, a man of slight stature and pale complexion. He peered over the tops of his glasses with baleful eyes, studying John and the unfriendly spectators, it seemed to me, as he might have studied customers as contracts were signed at the Levering automobile dealership in Los Angeles, one of the most profitable in the nation, we had been told.

John Beecher started by explaining the function of a teacher. Then he stated, with simple but convincing reasoning, why he had not signed the Levering Oath. Even the clerks who had been shuffling back and forth stopped and listened attentively. Reporters scribbled rapid notes and news service cameras turned.

John continued, "The Levering Oath is a conspiracy against our Constitution."

At that point the chairman interrupted him. "Mr. Beecher, I'll ask you to withdraw that word 'conspiracy.'"

John countered, "I've been an English teacher and I choose words for their precise meanings. 'Conspiracy' is *exactly* what I mean! I will not withdraw the word!"

The chairman scowled and conferred with Assemblyman Dickey. "I say you'll withdraw the word, Mr. Beecher, and not only that, you'll apologize to Assemblyman Levering, who's sitting there, right in front of you. If you don't do as I say, I'll instruct the Sergeant-at-Arms to eject you!"

John did not hesitate. He refused again.

The Sergeant-at-Arms was instructed to escort John from the Capitol, which he did to the jeers and boos of the audience. The chairman was pounding his gavel and shouting for order, his face livid. I jumped to my feet and tried to speak, but I was shouted down.

When things had calmed down a bit, Herb Bisno was permitted to make a brief statement. He charged "that if such procedure by political test is pursued, if oaths are continued, not only will the University of California stand discredited, but the entire school system in California will be in danger of being blacklisted."

Marguerite and I left the hearing room, to join John out on the street.

Not one person other than Levering had testified for the constitutional amendment. The members of the Assembly Committee on Constitutional Amendments, each one a sponsor of the original Levering Oath and the constitutional amendment, voted a "do pass."

When ACA No. 9 came up for a vote in the Assembly, an attempt was made by Assemblyman George D. Collins, Jr., to strike out all the important language of the proposal and to substitute the ancient Ephebic Oath taken by the men of Athens. Collins' idea didn't succeed with the Assembly, and the California Senate voted a "do pass" without even a hearing. What was worse, the voters approved the addition of the oath to the state constitution in the fall of the following year!

John Beecher and Herb Bisno had tried at the hearing to explain, and obviously the assemblymen had not wanted to hear, that everyone, from far right to the far left, was equally harmed by the oath. We were witnessing the destruction of the Bill of Rights by radicals who called themselves conservatives, while conservatives (in the basic sense of support for the Bill of Rights), were being called radicals and were silenced. Who was the real enemy among us, one had to ask?

In fact, opposition to the oath had cut across all party affiliations. A socially prominent judge, Joseph Ransome Longacre of Orinda, refused an appointment to a municipal board rather than sign. He declared that he wanted to retain the freedom to join in a revolution against any possible future totalitarian American regime.[7] Many other thoughtful persons deplored the damage the oath had done. Unlike Judge Longacre, however, most did nothing more than that.

I couldn't postpone my military service any longer. My offer to resign my commission had been rejected. I considered refusing to serve, but decided against that course. So, on the day after my six-month deferment expired, I reported for duty at Fort Lawton, in Seattle, Washington. Marguerite and Nancy accompanied me at first, but later they went to San Diego to be with Marguerite's parents.

No more than an hour had passed after I reported for duty at Fort Lawton before I was ordered to sign the U.S. Attorney General's list of "subversive" organizations. I refused. A day or two later, I was permitted to sign a substitute document; it was forwarded to Washington and a copy was placed in my service record. This document read as follows:

94

CONFIDENTIAL—SECURITY INFORMATION. The undersigned declines the requirement to sign DD Form 98 and DD Form 98a. The undersigned believes that involuntary disavowal of political beliefs and associations is contrary to the American traditions of political liberty. Frank A. Rowe 1st Lt. 0447539 Infantry.

Surely this would not be the only result of my refusal to sign the attorney general's list. At that moment I was fresh from the emotional turmoil of California's anti-Communist hysteria. I was no longer a civilian but a soldier subject to courts-martial, I was a long way from home and friends, and I was apprehensive about the Army's next move.

The Army sent me from Fort Lawton to Georgia for a one-month "refresher" course in infantry tactics. The class was made up of lieutenants and captains, all involuntarily recalled to active duty. I had reason to think that the officer in the next bunk was reporting the conversations I had with him, so I was careful to avoid names when he asked about my former life in California. Forty-nine of my classmates (out of fifty) went to combat in Korea at the end of that month. Much to my surprise, I was given orders to Fort Richardson, Alaska. Back in Fort Lawton, enroute to Alaska, Army Intelligence tried to interrogate me. I discussed the principle of the oath fight, but refused to say more. Nothing else happened.

As the heavily laden DC–4 cargo plane to which I was assigned flew over the fog-shrouded coast of British Columbia, I wondered if my Alaska assignment had been entirely a matter of chance.

It didn't seem unlikely, when I recalled the efforts by Army Intelligence and the FBI to question me about my civilian activities in California, that some staff officer may have thought that I would demoralize our combat troops. And perhaps the U.S. Army had not heard of the very efficient system used by totalitarian governments for getting rid of political unreliables— sending them into the hottest combat. In any case, I found a momentary peace in the steady drone of the big engines as we winged through the night toward Alaska.

I was assigned to a special services office, where I learned to organize a softball tournament and to manage a movie theater. On cold nights when I wasn't on duty, I would lie on my bed in the Bachelor Officer Quarters, play a scratchy *Roses of Picardy* or *Valse Triste* on my inexpensive phonograph, drink a bit too much, and think about how much I preferred Alaska to Korea.

I was honorably discharged in November 1952. I returned to our Alabama Street flat in San Francisco, where Marguerite and Nancy were waiting for me. Once home, I received a letter from the Secretary of the Army, in which he expressed gratitude for the contribution I had made to our country's freedom. I thought, "Now that I'm a civilian again, maybe I can *really* get to work on that."

Chapter 12

I CONTACTED SOME OF THE NONSIGNERS after my return from Alaska. Dr. Eason Monroe had been appointed executive director of the American Civil Liberties Union in Southern California, but many of the others were still unemployed or underemployed.

Some of the nonsigners were trying to make ends meet with underpaid jobs completely unrelated to their training. One was an auto parts salesman, another worked in a dress factory, still another sold encyclopedias. My first job after Alaska was in a silk-screen printing shop, a position I took in the futile hope that it might be close to my art interests. Our biggest commission turned out to be printing mobiles for a major wine company. Aside from their unattractive design, I learned that most were printed as a tax write-off and then destroyed. Only Herb Bisno had found another teaching post, at the University of Oregon.

There had been one suicide as a result of the Levering Oath. Another tragedy to affect some nonsigners was the breakup of the family. John Beecher and his wife had divorced after his dismissal. I suppose she could not appreciate what must have seemed his quixotic behavior. John's separation from his wife and family was devastating to him. I recall that he came to our Albama Street flat one morning so despondent that I feared he might harm himself. I tried to perk him up by drawing a quick charcoal portrait, but his mood showed in my picture so I destroyed it.

John had married again by the time I returned to Alabama Street. His new wife, Joan Stuck, was a former leader of the Student Committee for Academic Freedom. They moved to a ranch near Sebastopol where they tried to raise sheep and chickens and a garden.[1] Joan and John had thought they would adjust to ranch life, but Joan was the first to discover that she couldn't and she left for the East. John hung on for a time, but he eventually sold his "Morning Star" ranch to Lou Gottlieb of the Limelighter Singers. (It later became a much publicized commune in which the mores of middle-class society were conspicuously flouted.)

Aside from the news of old friends, we learned that important things had happened in the courts while I was away. In October 1952, the California Supreme Court upheld the Levering Oath in the matter of *Pockman* v. *Leonard*. The United States Supreme Court refused to consider Pockman's appeal of that ruling. *Frazer* v. *Regents* was also argued before the state's highest court, resulting in the rejection of the former UCLA teacher's plea.

But the California Supreme Court had upheld Professor Tolman in his suit against the University of California Regents. This decision permitted the rehiring of the university employees who had refused to sign the disclaimer oath, but many of them were teaching elsewhere, and in any case they would have had to sign the Levering Oath. Governor Warren's argument, that special oaths should not single out the academic community while other public employees were not required to bare their political beliefs, had been sustained. Now, all public employees, including the university teachers, were required to say that they did not now, never had, and never would belong to organizations that advocate overthrow of the government! Nothing had been accomplished for academic freedom by all of the court action. The victory achieved with *Tolman* v. *Underhill* had been negated by the Levering Oath.

The biggest setback in late 1952 occurred in November. I had returned from Alaska just in time to vote. The witch-hunting

legislators had succeeded in placing their constitutional amendment containing the Levering Oath on the ballot, and the voters
approved it. With the oath an integral part of the state constitution, any effort to do away with it in the future would
be extremely difficult.

On the national scene, an oppressive concern with political
heresy had hung over the elections in the fall of 1952. Presidential
candidate Dwight D. Eisenhower was silent about McCarthyism
(even though he told his close advisors that he loathed the man),
but his promise to go to Korea to patch up General MacArthur's
blunders appealed to the voters.[2] Eisenhower's "boy," vice-
presidential candidate Richard Nixon, made his famous
"Checkers speech" in 1952. His tearful explanation of questionable campaign fund-raising activities persuaded Eisenhower to
keep him as his running mate. With that crisis behind him, Nixon
reminded his audiences of the subversion that he perceived on
every hand and that the Democratic candidate for the presidency,
Adlai E. Stevenson, had been friendly with Alger Hiss.

Marguerite and I voted for Vincent Hallinan, the
San Francisco attorney who had spoken on the nonsigners' behalf
and who had defended some nonsigners in court. In that year, he
was the Progressive Party candidate for president. The party
was still alive even after six years of Red-baiting.

The name of Senator Joe McCarthy was in every newscast.
"Twenty years of treason" was the cowardly charge that
McCarthy used again and again to sow distrust. The recklessness
of charges levelled against loyal Americans in McCarthy's hey-
day was shown by an earlier incident. Mrs. Anna Rosenberg was
a brilliant lawyer whom President Truman had selected to be
Assistant Secretary of Defense. She was pilloried by Gerald L. K.
Smith, the antisemitic pamphleteer, by broadcaster Fulton Lewis,
Jr., and by J. B. Matthews, another dedicated "Commie" hunter.
They all maintained that she was a member of the reportedly
Communist John Reed Club. Only after she underwent weeks of
agony was it discovered there was indeed an Anna Rosenberg on
the West Coast who belonged to the club. The presidential
appointee Anna Rosenberg was finally confirmed.

McCarthy's influence was so great by the fall of 1952 that even Dwight Eisenhower was persuaded to delete a reference to his wartime commander, Chief of Staff George C. Marshall, when Eisenhower was campaigning in Wisconsin. Name-calling reached positively ridiculous proportions. Senator Robert Taft of Ohio, "Mr. Republican" to his colleagues, was called a Communist by a political opponent because Taft said he would favor federal aid for public housing.

McCarthyism affected lives in government, in education, in entertainment, indeed in every walk of life. Some time after McCarthy was finally censured by the Senate and after he had lurched drunkenly out of the scene to his death from kidney disease, actor Burgess Meredith remarked, "I had a personal stake in the era of fear that McCarthy generated. For two years I was not permitted to work in TV because of the blacklisters who ruled the networks in the 1950s." Twenty-five years after his blacklisting, Meredith would be given the role of Boston attorney Joseph Welch (Welch had been McCarthy's able adversary in the Army-McCarthy hearings), in a TV version of the rise and fall of Joe McCarthy.

A few of McCarthy's targets, such as Senator Margaret Chase Smith, survived his attacks by their dignified refusal to panic. In fact, Senator Smith treated him rather as if he were an adult delinquent. Most others were not so politic, and in many cases, lives and careers were ruined. Republican Senator Charles E. Potter described the time in very few words. As a member of the Senate Government Operations Committee, he wrote, "The McCarthy episode was, short of war, one of the most dramatic and provocative events in this century if not in all American history. It is unlikely that fate will ever again assemble a similar cast or write a comparable script."[4] Senator Potter made this statement before Watergate, of course. Nevertheless, few who experienced the McCarthy years would disagree.

For me, the lowest point of the inquisitorial McCarthy years, at least symbolically, was the execution of Julius and Ethel Rosenberg in Sing Sing on June 19, 1953. It seemed impossible that the evidence could have convicted them of giving atomic

100

bomb secrets to the Soviet Union or, as the judge who sentenced them to death charged, caused the Communist attack in Korea. Julius had been only an average student and Ethel had dropped out of school in her fifteenth year with hopes of a singing career. Facts, if one went beyond scare headlines, indicated that Julius and Ethel Rosenberg had been condemned by Ethel's brother David Greenglass, a somewhat incompetent machinist, and by the testimony of Harry Gold, a self-confessed liar.

However, after all the years of antiradical propaganda, hysteria about atomic and hydrogen bombs, loyalty purges, and congressional investigations, there was little wonder that protests against the scheduled executions were dismissed as the work of subversives intent on undermining "our way of life." Still, despite this accusation, many thousands of persons demonstrated on the Rosenbergs' behalf in the streets of major cities throughout the world.

In the Berkeley silk-screen shop where I worked, I heard the radio bulletins throughout the afternoon of the executions. I listened in horror as Julius Rosenberg, then Ethel Rosenberg, walked the last steps to the electric chair. The newscaster said the pair went to their deaths with a composure that astonished the witnesses. Ethel's last mortal act was to embrace the matron who had led her to the chair.

More stories came over the radio as I drove home from the shop. The sun was bright orange-red behind the San Francisco skyline. On that evening I saw the sunset as a symbol of the fear that the Rosenberg case had created. I recalled something I had read. I wasn't certain who had said it, but the essence was that for every martyr killed by oppression, two fighters would arise to destroy the oppressor.

That evening I went to the California Labor School. I had taken an occasional interest in its classes ever since we had moved to the Bay Area. The school had become an obvious target of the witch-hunters, as had the Jefferson School of Social Research in New York, the Seattle Labor School, and Communist Party-endorsed schools in other cities. In response to dwindling budgets and Red-baiting, the school had moved three times since my first

contact with it at its lower Market Street location. For several years, the school was in the building that is now a YMCA on Golden Gate Avenue, and at the moment of the Rosenberg executions in 1953, the California Labor School occupied the second floor of a tacky Victorian building on Divisadero Street. I had always felt a particularly strong tie to Giacomo Patri, the very human chairman of the school's art department for many years.

What depression! The San Francisco weather, cold and fog following quickly on the sunset, was dreary enough — without the news of that day. The mood of the people at the school that night was a combination of dejection and anger. I determined to do more to support the beleaguered school in the future. A few days later, I talked with Dr. Holland Roberts, the director.[5] We scheduled a children's art class for Saturday mornings. My class became a popular part of the curriculum. There children could do whatever they wished with poster paints, linoleum, or other donated art materials, or they could take part in painting wall-sized murals depicting events in progressive history.

It wasn't much when one recalls that the parents of some of my students were threatened with imprisonment, deportation, and at the least blacklisting and unemployment, but I'm proud of the teaching I did at the school. I've heard occasionally from some of the children (at the time of this writing in their thirties),

and I'll always think of them as children of the Rosenberg tragedy.

No hearing had ever been held on the dismissal of the nonsigners from State in 1950. Those registered letters stating that we were guilty of "gross unprofessional conduct" had been our only notice. But in 1953, the State Personnel Board acted to tidy up this obvious slighting of our constitutional right to due process. Several administrative oversights occurred during 1950–51 that could have had serious legal implications later. The lack of a hearing—a clear denial of the right to due process—was an obvious instance of such an oversight.

I received letters from the Personnel Board and from attorney Wayne Collins informing me that a hearing would be held on August 25, 1953. Evidently Collins or his secretary had forgotten that I, along with John Beecher, had dismissed him as our counsel in November 1950, and it seemed that Mr. Dreyfus had never informed the Personnel Board that he had become our attorney. In any case, along with eight of the nine San Francisco State nonsigners, I was notified and acknowledged receipt of the notice. Apparently, no one noticed that John's name was not on the list, and therefore no one communicated with him at his Sebastopol ranch.

The fact remains that John Beecher never received notice and has never had a hearing. To my nonlegal mind, a more serious

violation of the Fifth Amendment guarantee of due process
can hardly be imagined.

Mr. Collins was out of town and Mr. Dreyfus couldn't
accompany me on the hearing date. I went to the state building at
the appointed hour to demand a continuance until my counsel
could be present. A Mr. Gregory was the hearing officer.
I walked out when he told me that he would not delay the
proceeding. Attorney Lawrence Speiser, who had been hastily
summoned when it was learned that Mr. Collins would not be
there, requested that Leonard Pockman, Eason Monroe, Herb
Bisno, Lucy Hancock, and Phiz Mezey be allowed to resign
rather than be dismissed. By resigning, the stigma of refusing to
sign an oath would not be in their personnel records. (On the other
hand, I argued that resignation would make it impossible for one
to demand reinstatement when the oath was found to be unconstitutional, as it undoubtedly would.) In any case, a delay was
granted for the five, but after only a day or two, the resignation
idea was not allowed. In addition to myself, John Beecher,
Charlotte Howard, and Jack Patten did not appear. Thus,
our dismissals were made official.

Damage to my legal status that might have resulted
from walking out of the hearing was offset later by the proven
unconstitutionality of the oath. But it is difficult to think that
I might have acted differently even if I had been more aware of
legalisms. In 1953, the futility of any challenge to the Levering
Oath was overwhelming.

But perhaps it did not appear to be overwhelming to
two brave assemblymen who, in response to our urging, actually
introduced a bill to repeal the Levering Oath. The cosponsors
were Edward Elliott of Los Angeles and George D. Collins, Jr.,
of San Francisco. Assemblyman Collins, in particular, had never
missed a chance to point out the dangers to freedom inherent
in the oath. Assemblymen Hawkins, McMillan, and Condon
promised us that they would support the repeal bill.

At a hearing on the repeal bill, Assemblyman Levering
defended his brainchild by saying he would be willing to take
the oath "every morning before breakfast, if necessary."

"Loyalty 'oats' before breakfast" became a favorite pun in
our conversations.

The repeal bill died in committee and the efforts associated
with it may have only served to shorten the public careers of some
of the brave legislators who sponsored and supported it.

In spite of two recessions (1953–1954 and 1957–58),
the Republican campaign promises of peace and prosperity did
attain a certain validity for many people. The Korean War had
ended in a stalemate, suburbia blossomed, and upward mobility
accelerated. But one's point of view was all-important. In
retrospect, the 1953–1960 period was bleak; we seemed without
purpose other than to sustain ourselves. It was a time not unlike
political exile. Minorities still didn't share equally in the general
affluence, we lived under the constant threat of nuclear annihila-
tion, and we couldn't forget the careers that had been destroyed
by McCarthyism.

When another daughter, Georgia, was born in September
1953, we moved to Santa Rosa. As we drove away from our
Alabama Street flat, I saw a white sedan pull out, to follow us
about five car lengths behind during the entire fifty-mile distance
to our new home. Not long thereafter, we moved to Sacramento,
still followed by our government. The jobs I held in this period
were boring and socially nonproductive, but I learned enough
about silk-screen printing, display, and advertising layout to
provide for us. I even wrote a manual about display technique,
which brought us a little income and is still in print.

Marguerite and I were almost completely alienated from
efforts to repeal the oath by then. We assumed that there were
probably still those who would claim that they were resisting from
"within the system." We considered this a hypocritical attitude,
and on the rare occasions when we met such people socially, our
intransigence about the oath embarrassed them. Businessmen
who were my nine-to-five associates every day parroted the
platitudes of the Eisenhower prosperity or, more often, had no
opinions at all beyond the sales for the day compared with the
figure for the same day the previous year. And in those years,
figures almost always showed a "gain."

But were sales gains a source of happiness? In the late 1950s, it seemed to me that the entire nation was being crushed by mediocrity, dull routine, and prejudice. The prejudices were racial, and against women, socialism, and minority opinion in general. And little evidence existed to suggest that an awakening would ever take place. Several small political parties claimed to have the necessary program, but, to me, they seemed more intent on fighting each other than the system. The Communist Party USA, in spite of protestations of its leaders that the party shared a philosophy but nothing more with the Soviet Communists, seemed too complacent in the face of obvious horrors in the "Socialist paradise."

The "Doctors' Plot" of 1952, in which a large group of Kremlin doctors, most of them Jewish, were imprisoned for allegedly trying to poison Soviet leaders, seemed to me a clear indication that antisemitism existed in the Soviet Union, but our few acquaintances in the Communist Party didn't want to talk about that. The Hungarian uprising that followed the death of Stalin and its violent suppression by the Red Army may have caused many defections from the CPUSA, but too many people, it seemed, used the cliché, "You can't make an omelette without breaking eggs," or other rationalizations to excuse tyranny.

By the time of the Twentieth Congress and Khrushchev's revelation of the Stalinist terror, defection from the Communist Party had increased dramatically. From the War Against Fascism until 1957, CPUSA membership dropped from approximately eighty thousand to ten thousand.[6] Of course, some people left the party by expulsion and some left because of the incessant persecution of the party and its leaders, but many left, it seemed to me, because they became disillusioned.

During the late 1950s, I applied to many school systems in states that still didn't require special oaths as well as to privately endowed schools in California. On every application I had to state that I had been fired from my last position because I had refused to sign a loyalty oath. Of course, offers were few and far between, two to be precise. (Later, John Beecher, the former sociology professor from State, told me that in response to one of his employment applications, he had been told that hiring a paroled convict would be easier than hiring him.) One offer would have given us an income far below the standard for a family of four. The other would have disrupted our family life (Nancy was student body president of her school at the time) because a move to a distant state would have been required. I turned the offers down and we stayed busy with the children's school activities, my job, and occasionally a little art. Contact with old friends in the Bay Area became rare. From time to time, however, incidents in the news reminded us of the continuing offensive against academic freedom in the California schools.

Richard E. Combs, chief counsel for the State Fact-Finding Committee on Un-American Activities, proudly announced that former FBI agents would be installed on many university campuses and in local school systems, their salaries paid by the taxpayers. Their instructions would be to report the political activities of teachers directly to counsel Combs.

Associate Professor of Psychology Dr. Harry C. Steinmetz was dismissed by San Diego State University under provisions of the Luckel Act for refusing to say if he was a Communist. Said Dr. Steinmetz, "The revelation of weakness, ignorance, and social indifference among most academic colleagues quite turned me around."

John and Inez Schnigten, teachers in Richmond, refused to answer questions of the state Un-American Activities Committee and were fired under provisions of the Dilworth Act.

John W. Mass, an English instructor at San Francisco City College, was called to a San Francisco hearing by HUAC, where he admitted he had been a Communist when he signed the Levering Oath but refused to say more, as was his privilege under the Fifth Amendment. The college invoked the Dilworth Act to dismiss him, but Mr. Mass took the matter to court and became one of the few teachers of that period to fight back successfully. He was reinstated and awarded back pay in 1956.

One and all, the professors, the preachers, and the editors, hold their jobs by serving the Plutocracy. . . .

Jack London, *The Iron Heel*, 1907

Chapter 13

ONE MORNING IN JUNE 1957, we sat down to breakfast and were greeted by a familiar face on the front page of the *Chronicle*.[1] Jack Patten, the English instructor who had been at San Francisco State, had dropped from sight in early 1951, having used most of the little bit of money the Student Committee for Academic Freedom had collected to help the nonsigners. At that time, he had said he needed it because of an illness in his family.

Now he had resurfaced as an informer for the House Committee on Un-American Activities, the most pitiful role of all the dramatis personae in the anti-Communist dramas. Typical procedure for committee investigators was to find someone with a flaw in their past, such as alcoholism or debts perhaps, but usually the possible violation of any of the numerous antisubversive statutes—whatever might make them vulnerable. Then, by gentle coaching the committee would convince the person to name former friends and colleagues rather than be prosecuted. The deal was almost always worked out in advance, in executive sessions.

At a HUAC hearing in San Francisco City Hall, Patten testified that he had at one time belonged to the Communist Party, but had left when he underwent psychiatric treatment. He named people he had allegedly known within the Party ranks. Most of the people Patten fingered as former comrades refused to respond to his charges, invoking the Fifth Amendment, but Tom Hardwick, who had been a teacher at Burlingame High, talked back defiantly.[2] When Hardwick was asked by Chairman Francis E. Walter if he was aware that Patten had said he was a Communist, he shot back, "He also said he was undergoing psychiatric treatment when he thought he knew me!"

The HUAC hearing became a shameful circus, with charges recklessly thrown about. On the day following Patten's testimony, a broadcaster for KCBS was fired by the network for refusing to answer the committee's questions. But the most tragic incident of the 1957 HUAC hearing had happened two days before the session opened.

A forty-one-year-old Stanford University research scientist, William K. Sherwood, had died, an apparent suicide. He had been subpoenaed by HUAC. Mr. Sherwood had told his wife, "I'm going to end it all. I'm going to kill myself." At that moment she did not think her husband was in earnest. When he hadn't returned home from the Hopkins Marine Laboratory by midnight, police were called, and Sherwood was found dying of self-administered poison.

Mr. Sherwood left a letter in which he stated, "My life and my livelihood are now threatened by the House committee . . . . I will be in two days assassinated by publicity . . . . I would love to spend the next few years in laboratories and I would hate to spend

them in jail."

When he died, the young scientist had been working on a project through which he believed he had found a possible physical link between cancer, some of the heart diseases, and schizophrenia.

Frank Tavenner, the investigator for HUAC, confirmed that Sherwood had been subpoenaed but refused to discuss how Sherwood might have been involved in anything subversive. Of course, he and Chairman Walter denied any responsibility for the suicide. Mr. Sherwood's widow wanted to address the committee. When her request was denied, she distributed a statement to the spectators that said in part, "Members of the committee, what you have done is an evil thing. Do not persist in it. Go away, go home, bow your heads in prayer and ask forgiveness of God."[3]

It was later learned that the committee may have wanted to question Sherwood about work he had done with the Board of Economic Warfare in Rio de Janeiro during the War Against Fascism. Someone had alleged that Sherwood possessed "certain books and had Negro friends."

John Beecher's poem about the incident expressed many people's feelings:

Inquest
A man lies dead today who yesterday
was working in his laboratory. He killed
himself. Killing himself he killed far more
besides. His research centered on the link
between twin scourges of mankind, cancer
and schizophrenia. This died with him.
Who knows what else? And all for what good end?
The man lies dead and cannot be subpoenaed
even by the Committee but awaits
that judgement which the Congressmen themselves
will someday stand to. He was accused of what?
Of nothing. If you prefer, of everything
that wild surmise can dream or sickest mind
invent. No fire in all the smoke? This much
perhaps, that in his youth he was deceived

110

by some who promised to redress world wrong.
(The Constitution left him free to make
his own mistakes.) Now, deep in career
of dedicated service to mankind
he must confess, recant his early errors,
inform on friends whose guilt was no more real
than was his own. Or he must choose the way
of silence while men break him on the wheel
of public degradation, his sweating face
on television screens across the land,
a super-pillory where all may mock
and spit at him, his wife and children shamed
in every circle where they move, and then
the ultimate; his scientific work
halted, himself without a job or hope
of finding one, his family destitute . . . .
and so he took the poison. What would you
have had him do, gentlemen of the Committee?[4]

And then the tide slowly began to turn. As tiny riffles appear on the surface of the sea as the ebb begins, so could we see the change of sentiment against disclaimer oaths.

A 1956 court ruling had ordered that back salaries be paid to the University of California teachers who had defied the Regents' Oath. One of the nonsigners of 1949, David Saxon, was later to become a vice chancellor and, still later, president of that great institution.

In 1960, the California Supreme Court ruled that an unemployed person who turned down a public job because of conscientious objection to the Levering Oath could collect unemployment benefits. This ruling was quickly followed by two more, one negating the requirement that organizations had to sign the oath before they could use a public school building for any kind of meeting, and the second affirming that a Methodist Church in San Leandro and the First and the Valley Unitarian Universalist Churches in Los Angeles could not be denied tax exemptions for failure to subscribe to the oath. The latter stemmed from a 1952 amendment to the California Constitution, which allowed tax exemptions to be claimed only by those who

111

did not advocate the violent overthrow of the government. The revenue code had been amended in 1953 to require all who applied for property tax exemptions to sign the Levering Oath.

One day in 1960, I strolled along the Sacramento River on a rare afternoon off and then stopped at the library to browse. Late in the afternoon, I stopped for a haircut. The radio was tuned to the news and an announcer said something about a riot at San Francisco City Hall. Police and firemen had ejected students from another hearing of the House Un-American Activities Committee. The barber handed me a newspaper that confirmed the story. A picture showed police and firemen at the top of the steps, firehoses at full blast, with students in tattered jeans tumbling head over heels down the steps.

The barber asked what I thought. I said, "Aren't they beautiful . . . . but where were they in 1950?" The barber frowned. I think he didn't know if I was referring to the students or the cops.

Students had at last emerged from their apathy, and at San Francisco City Hall! As they were to demonstrate over and over again during the decade to come — in the Berkeley Free Speech movement, in the drive for the rights of black citizens in Mississippi, and during the Vietnam War — young militants refused to exclude allies on the basis of ideology. Democrats, Republicans, Socialists, Communists, and persons without a party would be welcomed if they would work for the cause. One would not have to take an oath to march for peace and freedom. Factionalism, which had plagued the Left for decades, was to be set aside under the pressure of the greater imperatives of Selma and Vietnam.

We heard news of more nonsigners. Charles Aronson, a mathematics instructor at the University of California, and Barbara Garson, another university teacher, refused to sign the Levering Oath. Barbara Garson's statement to the press was particularly good:

Many of us have very sensitive moral stomachs and we gag on the oath. But by swallowing it down instead of spitting it out, we only make ourselves weaker and sicker. Once infected by this consciousness of compromise our condition continues to deteriorate. When we should be speaking up and organizing we say to ourselves, "I got my job through a compromise. Who am I to speak up like a hero?" And thus the oath selectively weakens that part of the campus community which might fight future indignities.[5]

By this time, Marguerite and I were so certain that I would be able to return to a teaching career that we gave up everything in Sacramento and moved back to the Bay Area, a very difficult thing for our children. I found another job and became a part-time student so I could take the graduate courses I would need to compete in the teacher job market. I had been concerned that my age might be a handicap in the Mills College graduate school. Instead, I found that I could do as well or better than younger students. In fact, I had the top score in the art history examination and was awarded the Trefethen Fellowship for my second semester of study. I completed my studies at the age of forty-six and was ready to work any time the Levering Oath was found unconstitutional.

A big break came when the United States Supreme Court invalidated the Washington State loyalty oath in 1964. Then two Arizona teachers, the Elfbrandts, challenged the special oath in their state. They continued to work without pay while their case went through the lower courts up to the United States Supreme Court, which, in late 1966, upheld their position. The Elfbrandts were reinstated and awarded back pay. Then, on January 24, 1967, New York's "anti-subversive" Feinberg Law was found unconstitutional by the United States Supreme Court.[6]

The only instance of prosecution for perjury under terms of the Levering Act occurred in the late 1960s and involved a husband and wife who had taught in Redding, California. The school board had fired Rita and William Mack on the ground that they had falsely stated that they were not Communists, even though they said they had quit the party in 1957, after the Hungarian uprising.

When the Macks sued for return of their teaching credentials, Judge Joseph Karesh of San Francisco Superior Court ruled in their favor. It had not been proven, according to Judge Karesh,

113

that the Macks knew that the Communist Party advocated the overthrow of the U.S. government when they signed the oath.[7] Judge Karesh, by basing his ruling on that narrow issue, just missed the distinction of being the judge to find the Levering Oath unconstitutional.

But eventually it did occur. On the evening of December 21, 1967, I returned late from an office Christmas party for the supermarket chain where I was the advertising manager.

When I opened the front door of our house, Marguerite, Nancy, and Georgia shouted in unison, "Guess what?"

I replied, "Don't keep me waiting. I give up!"

"The California Supreme Court has thrown out the oath!" was their joyous answer.

I could hardly control my emotions as they told me what they had heard on the late television news. The morning newspapers filled in the details. The case called *Vogel* v. *Los Angeles* had been filed by Dr. Eason Monroe and the attorneys at the American Civil Liberties Union of Southern California in early 1967. A lower court ruling for Vogel had been appealed to the California Supreme Court. The high court made clear in its December 21 opinion that the Levering Oath "is invalid because it bars persons from public employment for a type of association that may not be proscribed consistently with First Amendment rights."[8]

I sent congratulations to Dr. Monroe at the Southern California ACLU for leading us to this outstanding victory.

I also wrote to John Beecher to ask if he regretted anything. He replied from Massachusetts, where he was reading his poetry:

If I ever said that we might have been wrong about the oath it was in an ironical spirit because I have never thought that. As I told you, my sense of the correctness of our action has hardened into absolute certainty over the years. I wish I could say that about all the rest of my actions. But that is one thing I will stand by for eternity. I agree that, in the end, it made me a bigger person and helped my art incalculably. Maybe I will drop a wreath on Levering's grave when I come out there."

Assemblyman Harold K. Levering had died in August 1967. The obituary gave the facts: "Firm opponent of the union shop, indefatigable investigator of subversives during his fourteen years (1948–1962) as State Assemblyman from Santa Monica, Harold K. Levering, 72, was found shot in the right temple with a .25-caliber revolver, an apparent suicide, in his Bel-Air home."[9]

Legal rights acquire meaning only if enforced. The dignity of the higher education profession falters when those rights are permitted to be ignored on the campuses of California colleges and universities.

Peter Galiano, General Counsel
California Teachers Association

Chapter 14

THE RULING OF THE State Supreme Court might have had a still happier ending if our former colleagues, who had assured us they would resist the oath from *within* the system, had welcomed us after seventeen years of exile.

But because the people we had known at San Francisco State in 1950 did not exactly roll out the welcome mat (some had become highly placed administrators) or because they responded to our reinstatement inquiries as though the oath had never existed, the 1967 ruling of the California Supreme Court was not to be the end of the story.

At first, I assumed that the San Francisco State staff would rejoice in our victory with us. My letter of December 27 to President Summerskill shows the naive optimism I felt:

I am making plans to resume my teaching career that was interrupted by the Levering Oath. I'm certain you understand the happiness I felt when I learned about the court ruling. Now, I'm looking forward to the day when I can devote myself wholeheartedly to the vocation I have always cherished. May I have a personal interview at your earliest convenience?

If Dr. Summerskill understood my happiness, he was too absorbed with his own problems to give it much attention.[1]

In the fall of 1967, San Francisco State was gripped in a dispute that soon led to the greatest campus turbulence in American history and forced Summerskill to resign. The next

116

president of the university was Robert Smith. He was soon replaced by S.I. Hayakawa, the feisty "law and order" choice of the trustees.

Meanwhile, Dean Feder of Academic Planning replied to my letter as though I had never taught at San Francisco State. The only reason for my departure, the unconstitutional oath, was completely ignored:

Recommendations for the hiring of faculty members now originate in the department concerned. Hence, if the Department of Art does have need for someone with your special qualifications and abilities, I am certain they will want to be in touch with you.[2]

Five hundred arrests, dozens of injuries to students and police, bomb incidents, fires, and a partial faculty strike occurred at San Francisco State during the Hayakawa presidency.

The strike started with ten demands by the Black Students Union but was soon expanded to cover the wants of all ethnic minorities. The suspension of a black graduate teaching assistant who allegedly had told students to bring guns onto campus further inflamed passions. It wasn't exactly the calm atmosphere for discussion of my assignment that I had wished.

But the more I thought about the refusal of the administration even to acknowledge the principle we had defended, the more I determined to insist upon reinstatement and financial compensation. I considered placing an advertisement to contact nonsigners throughout the state who might wish to join in the class-action lawsuit. Upon reflection, this seemed impractical, so I settled for contacting as many of the San Francisco Bay Area people as possible. What I learned about them was discouraging.

Of the San Francisco State College nonsigners, Leonard Pockman and Charlotte Howard had died. Herbert Bisno was teaching at the University of Oregon and did not respond. Lucy Hancock seemed to be uninterested when I telephoned her.

Dr. Eason Monroe, the former chairman of the Division of Language Arts was, of course, director of the American Civil Liberties Union in Southern California. He had made a career of reinstatement and the overturn of the oath ever since his departure from San Francisco State, so there was no question about his wishes.

Phiz Mezey was a photojournalist and teacher in San Francisco. She was interested in a lawsuit but her reinstatement might be complicated since she had returned to teach at San Francisco State in 1965 while the oath was still a requirement for employment, and then had left again because of the strike.

John Beecher had married again after giving up his Sebastopol ranch, and had gone on to teach in Arizona and at Santa Clara University. He had his own letterpress which he used to publish his poetry. John was eager to sue, especially since he had once shared an office with S. I. Hayakawa when both men were instructors at the University of Wisconsin but Hayakawa had simply ignored his letters.

Jack Patten, the ex-English instructor and informer for the Un-American Activities Committee, couldn't be located.

My search for city and county workers, and teachers in elementary schools, high schools, and the junior college was only partially successful. Three former teachers had died. One had taught at San Francisco City College, one at a high school, and the third in an elementary school.

I recalled that one of the San Francisco elementary school teachers whom I couldn't locate had been drafted just about the time I was recalled into the Army.

One nonsigner had become an attorney and another, a former bus driver for San Francisco's municipal railroad, was preparing for the State Bar examination. A former high school teacher had married a prominent civil rights attorney.

Tom Hardwick, the former Burlingame High teacher who had bravely defied HUAC, had become a well-known labor union official. A popular commentator on radio station KPFA was Adam David Miller, who had refused to sign the oath as an Oakland hospital worker. If nothing else, my survey certainly showed that the nonsigners had been resourceful.

Ann Rosenfield, who had been secretary of the Joint Action Council, was in social work and lived in Walnut Creek. Beb Bratt, who had been our treasurer, had retired. Mort Elkins, who had visited the Carricos with us, was also in social work with Thelma Harris, now Mrs. Elkins.

A few of the people I contacted had already made inquiries about getting their jobs back. The outlook wasn't bright. The reply was always the same, that only those who had held some kind of tenure in 1950 had a chance, and then only if they fought their cases through long and expensive lawsuits.

In fact, a few legislators even seemed bent on reviving the issue. Assemblyman Hayes from Long Beach introduced a constitutional amendment that he thought would make the disclaimer oath acceptable to the courts by making a few minor changes in the wording of the oath. He couldn't arouse enough interest in his idea however, and it was defeated.

My efforts to find legal assistance began immediately after the December 1967 court ruling. I wrote, telephoned, and visited attorneys in their offices. The Dreyfus firm informed me, "We feel the chances for success in such litigation would be too small to warrant undertaking it."[3] I was met with pessimism or disinterest wherever I inquired.

Attorneys who had complimented me in 1950 for my dedication to the Bill of Rights seemed to be occupied with more important matters in 1968.

Marguerite and I have always been proud that we marched

119

in every major Bay Area anti-Vietnam War demonstration. We had also participated in civil rights demonstrations, but we couldn't help feeling a trace of bitterness when our story fell on deaf ears. We knew as we made posters and marched, that the monstrous war and the terrible racism were but the logical results of the silent years—years that had been partially shaped by the unconstitutional oath.

In each of my futile visits to law offices I had offered to enter into a contingency arrangement that would have given the attorney a large part of any damages collected. The only offer I received from a lawyer in the first months of 1968 was to research the matter for a fee (I believe $500 was suggested) with no promise to proceed if the chance of success appeared slight. It seemed obvious that I would probably have forfeited my money.

In 1950, the small teacher's union at San Francisco State had had little effect in regard to the oath. Then, as now, the American Federation of Teachers, of which I am a member, had been more concerned with bread-and-butter issues than with constitutional principles or academic freedom. Nevertheless, the United Professors of California (AFT's name at state universities) was contacted but nothing came of this immediately, since the union's

budget and energies were completely claimed by the massive
strike that gripped the campus.

I continued to correspond with Dr. Eason Monroe, in his
position as executive director of the ACLU in Los Angeles. He
informed me that a suit for reinstatement and back pay would be
filed, but that his attorneys had advised him that only he should be
named as the petitioner. I appealed to Dr. Monroe and to his
attorney, Mr. Okrand, to include other nonsigners in the suit.
They insisted that the Monroe case, if successful, would serve as
precedent for others, but that it would be best if the petitioner
had held tenure at the time of dismissal. Of course I was
disappointed.

About the pending case Dr. Monroe wrote, "I am not
terribly optimistic about winning, but my lawyers have done a
first-rate job of presenting the case. Who knows, we may all be
back at San Francisco State before the end of this century."

I discussed my interest in the Monroe lawsuit with
Mr. Marshall Krause at the Northern California ACLU office.
I had been told that General Counsel Wayne Collins, who had
argued the unsuccessful Pockman case in court, had relinquished
many of his duties to this younger man. Mr. Krause had represented the Macks in their successful 1967 suit to recover their
teaching credentials. Mr. Krause was nice about it, but he told me
I would have to find someone else to represent myself and other
nonsigners; he agreed with the strategy outlined by his colleagues
in Southern California.

My anger was beginning to rise. I wondered where all the
lawyers were who had always said the oath was such an affront.

After a few weeks I returned to the ACLU office to learn
that Mr. Krause was no longer there and that the new counsel was
Mr. Paul Halvonik, a young, urbane former staff counsel. Mr.
Halvonik repeated the gist of our conversation in a letter intended
to help me understand the legal intricacies of the matter:

It is your opinion that your lack of tenured status has not the slightest
bearing on the justice of your case. I could not agree more. But that is
not the point. Lack of tenure does have a significant legal bearing on

your case. *Law and justice are not the same thing.* [Italics are mine.] If they were, you would not have been dismissed in the first place. We want to establish the legal principle that persons dismissed because of their refusal to execute the oath are entitled to reinstatement. The first case should be the strongest case, a case unburdened with extraneous considerations that may foreclose the possibility of establishing the principle at all.[4]

Mr. Halvonik did volunteer to ask a court to "expunge" my official employment record of any reference to "unprofessional conduct." I declined because I thought I had acted in the most professional way possible, by refusing to sign the unconstitutional oath. If any record required "expunging," I thought it should be San Francisco State's.

John Beecher was becoming increasingly impatient. He kept up a steady barrage of letters from his home in North Carolina or from wherever he was reading poetry at that moment. In one letter to me he deplored the lack of progress:

I hope you can find a lawyer who can tell the difference between legality and justice in our case although I am pretty dubious. The California Supreme Court is certainly not going to take a different view of our claims than of Eason's, and I suppose it is questionable whether that court would even sustain our rights to reinstatement. Probably not, since none of us had tenure in 1950. What would we do then, take it up to the U.S. Supreme Court and expect to get justice from Chief Justice Burger, Mr. Justice Rehnquist, Mr. Justice Powell and others of the Nixonized bench?

I was fully occupied in 1968. In addition to my reinstatement efforts, I was still ad manager of a twenty-eight-unit supermarket chain, a deadline job full of pressures. The time I took to plead with lawyers had to be made up at night. Also, much time was consumed by the applications I was making to other schools when it became obvious that San Francisco State would not have me back without a struggle.

It was a happy day for Marguerite and me when my efforts resulted in a job at Laney College in Oakland. The energetic chairman of the art department, Roger Ferragallo, interviewed me and said I could start teaching in the Spring 1969 semester, eighteen long years after my dismissal at San Francisco State.

My new job gave me a better chance to interest teacher organizations in the case. My local, 1603, Peralta Federation of Teachers, endorsed those of us who had been dismissed. I was confident, in the last months of 1969 and throughout 1970, that justice would eventually be achieved.

In all my conversations with Dr. Monroe, Mr. Halvonik, and other attorneys, no one had mentioned that, to protect my rights, I had to file a claim with the State Board of Control. Perhaps I had heard of the board, but I thought then that it had to do with liquor sales or something.

The function of the Board of Control, I soon learned, was to rule upon the claims of Californians who believe they have suffered losses because of actions of the state. The board rules on all sorts of matters, from minor accidents to wrongful discharge from state employment.

In any case, Phiz Mezey, John Beecher, and I received letters from Dr. Monroe, with a copy of Monroe's claim to use as a guide and the suggestion that we also file claims. I estimated what I would have earned if I had remained at San Francisco State from 1950, subtracted what I actually had earned in the same time period, and this became the amount of my claim. But by the time we received Monroe's letter, it was physically impossible to assemble, notarize, and mail the necessary documents before the deadline. Mr. Halvonik kindly gave me a statement that he had not advised me about the claim procedure,[5] but it did no good. We would have to try again at a later date and perhaps be turned down because of statutory limits.

The same letter from Dr. Monroe conveyed the good news that Mr. Okrand had filed a lawsuit in Los Angeles Superior Court on behalf of Phiz Mezey, John Beecher, and Frank Rowe. However, Mr. Okrand cautioned everyone that this case would not be pressed until a ruling had been made on the Monroe case.

On March 17, 1971, *Monroe* v. *Trustees* was argued before the Court of Appeal in Los Angeles and the opinion was forwarded to the California Supreme Court.

The first twenty-one pages of the Supreme Court ruling dealt with whether or not Dr. Monroe had filed suit within the time defined by law, and whether or not his action accrued from 1950 or from 1967. On page 22, the judges got into what I believed to be the issue:

The Nation's future depends upon leaders trained through wide exposure to that robust exchange of ideas which discovers truth "out of a multitude of tongues, rather than through any authoritative selection." The reinstatement of petitioner, *and other similarly situated teachers* [italics are mine] will serve to broaden, and thereby enrich, the academic community by reintroducing into that community individuals with conscientiously held beliefs and ideals, beliefs which in the past have been excluded from the public schools simply because of public disapproval.[6]

On December 30, 1971, the California Supreme court ruled in Dr. Monroe's favor.

If other teachers were "similarly situated," to use the Supreme Court's phrase, subsequent events didn't show it.

I urged the American Civil Liberties Union to proceed with the Mezey, Beecher, and Rowe lawsuit now that the "strong" case had been won. Marguerite and I went to Los Angeles to talk directly with Dr. Monroe and Mr. Okrand, but they said that it would not be that easy. All of the usual reasons for possible failure, lack of tenure, the statute of limitations, etc., etc., were patiently explained to us. I replied that I didn't give a damn about legalisms, that all I could see was the injustice. I had been dismissed for no reason other than the oath, the oath had been declared unconstitutional, not once but twice, *so why couldn't I have my job back*?

Dr. Monroe's return to the San Francisco State campus was widely reported but there was not a hint in the newspapers that others might be awaiting reinstatement. President Hayakawa made the best of what I am certain he considered a bad situation, and welcomed Dr. Monroe with cordiality.

Dr. Eason Monroe died not long after his return to the school he had left twenty-two years earlier, a victim of lung cancer. Without his untiring efforts, as leader of the Federation for Repeal of the Levering Act, and as the initiatior of *Vogel* v. *County of*

Los Angeles, the lawsuit that overturned the oath in the first instance, everything else that has happened by way of justice for the nonsigners would have been delayed until a much later time.

So with the Monroe decision, a new phase of the run-around with San Francisco State University opened (the name was changed from college to university at about that time). Whenever an important official was replaced, and the changes were quite rapid in the hectic strike period, I immediately dispatched a letter to remind the administration of my continued desire for reinstatement.

Through Phiz Mezey's efforts, we met with the UPC Academic Freedom Committee, a standing committee of the United Professors of California, soon after the Monroe decision, and the UPC agreed to sponsor us. Two members of the San Francisco State faculty, Nancy McDermid and Eric Solomon, were especially effective in presenting our case to that committee, and soon thereafter Mr. Okrand transferred the suit, which had been languishing in Los Angeles Superior Court, to the Superior Court in San Francisco. Victor Van Bourg, for the United Professors of California, would represent us.

Mr. Van Bourg is senior partner in one of the largest labor law firms in Northern California. He is very proud of his labor heritage, his father having been a Painters Union organizer, first in New York and later in Los Angeles. He has been the able spokesman for San Francisco city employees in many cases. San Francisco teachers and employees of the Bay Area Rapid Transit system have also been represented by attorneys in the Van Bourg firm.

At our only interview, Phiz Mezey, Marguerite, and I waited in the anteroom while staff attorneys went in and out of Van Bourg's office. When we were finally seated before his desk, Van Bourg conferred with still another attorney on the telephone while I studied a framed Farm Workers poster, with *Huelga* in bold red letters, behind his sturdy, bearded head. At last, Mr. Van Bourg shifted his large, muscular body forward in his chair and asked a few questions. Then he dismissed us, with a comment that he would see what could be done. I left his office hoping that, at last, we would have our day in court.

Months passed before we were called by Mr. Stewart Weinberg, the Van Bourg staff attorney assigned to our case. He started the interview by outlining a few of the legal hurdles we would face. Many accounts of Mr. Weinberg's excellent and often successful defenses of teachers had been printed in my union newspaper. One was a report of his championing one hapless fellow who had been fired for using a publication called the *Inner City Mother Goose* in his classroom.[7] An incensed parent had demanded that the teacher be fired for immorality because *Mother Goose* contained a certain four-letter word. While I felt that issue was perhaps not as basic as ours, I was certain that Mr. Weinberg would represent us with equal skill. He took a few notes and said we would hear from him.

Almost a year passed. The Van Bourg office sent me copies of strong letters that Mr. Weinberg had addressed to the counsel representing San Francisco State. I felt we were in good hands. Then, one day, I was astounded by a letter from Mr. Weinberg, informing me that the United Professors of California had retained another law firm to represent us. Soon thereafter, the chairman of the UPC Academic Freedom Committee confirmed that another law firm would handle the Beecher, Mezey, and Rowe case in the future. More months passed.

Late in 1973, I expressed my frustration in bitter letters to the chairman of the UPC Academic Freedom Committee and to our newly appointed attorney. I pointed out that any deadlines missed or legal steps not taken had been due to the insistence of Dr. Monroe's advisors at the American Civil Liberties Union and other attorneys that only formerly tenured persons stood much of a chance for reinstatement through legal action. I demanded to know why it was taking so long to get a hearing. Twenty-three years had passed since we'd been dismissed, six years had passed since California's highest court had found the Levering Oath unconstitutional, and almost two years had gone by since the California Supreme Court had ruled for the second time, in the Monroe case, that the oath was unconstitutional.

Now I wanted to know why we had to prove anything

at all. What more did the trustees of the university system and their administrators want? These same ladies and gentlemen who prattled about law and order had revealed themselves as hypocrites, since they ignored the rulings of the court and denied our repeated requests for reinstatement. To me, the refusal of the California State University and Colleges to recognize our rights was tantamount to acceptance of the Levering Oath and all that the oath implied.

In the UPC Academic Freedom Committee's reply to my letter, I was told that I had made a false and malicious statement about the UPC attorney, who also informed me that any further legal action would depend solely upon an "agreement upon the facts" between himself and the university counsel.

Chapter 15

AVING PRETTY MUCH GIVEN UP on the chance for redress in the courts, Marguerite and I took my case to John Knox, assemblyman for the 11th District, where Marguerite and I live. The principal cities in the district are Richmond, Martinez, and Pleasant Hill. A Democratic and liberal, Assemblyman Knox's district is a mixture of blue-collar and white-collar workers. Mr. Knox's opposition to the Levering Oath went clear back to 1950. At one point he had been chairman of the East Bay Committee for Repeal of the Levering Act. He told us he thought we could persuade the legislature to act favorably on a resolution.

It was during the 1975–76 session of the legislature that Knox informed us our resolution requesting the reinstatement of any State College nonsigners who desired it had been introduced in the State Assembly. The resolution was cosponsored by Assemblyman John Vasconcellos of San Jose, the chairman of the Assembly Committee on Higher Education. Even without a back-pay provision, which I had vigorously propounded, Assembly Concurrent Resolution 171 would certainly be the most positive thing that had happened since the State Supreme Court ruling of December 1967.[1]

After a number of paragraphs beginning with WHEREAS, the resolution read as follows:

In the years since the Monroe case, there has been little if any reinstatement by the Trustees of the California State University and

128

Colleges of persons wrongfully discharged for refusal to take the Levering Oath; now, therefore, be it

Resolved by the Assembly of the State of California, the Senate thereof concurring, that the Trustees of the California State University and Colleges are requested to report to the Legislature the names of all persons so discharged and their current employment situation, and whether they desire to be reinstated; and be it further
Resolved, That the trustees are requested to reinstate any persons so discharged, and who desire reinstatement; and be it further
Resolved, That a copy of this resolution be transmitted to the Trustees of the California State University and Colleges.

Marguerite and I went to Sacramento on June 24, 1976, for the hearing on ACR 171 before the Assembly Committee on Higher Education. Assemblymen Vasconcellos, an unconventional politician, in appearance at least, chaired the meeting. It started at 4 P.M., and our item was the last thing on the agenda. However, I had talked with Mr. Vasconcellos before the meeting opened. I suggested that the resolution be amended to allow for back pay and that it cover all nonsigners, not just former San Francisco State teachers. He said both requests were beyond the scope of his committee. I then decided not to insist on amendments, since ACR 171, as proposed, was indeed a step forward.

I knew that John Beecher had sent a letter to the committee, but if there were other expressions of support, they were not read. I had hoped that there might be a message from Governor Jerry Brown's office, where I had made appeals for reinstatement. I had even received a verbal expression of support from one of the governor's important aides, but, again, if such a message was sent, no announcement was made.

The members of the 1976 Assembly Committee on Higher Education were young and two were women. I believe only one, Assemblyman Collier, had been in the legislature in the McCarthy-Levering years. The major agenda items that afternoon concerned the rights of part-time teachers in the community college system. Representatives of teacher organizations spoke for or against a proposal to correct inequities in the part-timers' lot. After a vote to delay action, almost everyone left, including two members of the committee. It was 6:30 P.M. by that time, everyone was worn out, and one or two members said something about food. Assemblyman Vasconcellos called upon me to speak.

I outlined the story of the oath and of my efforts as lucidly as I could, and then a committee member asked a question. My reply was evidently too long because, when I asked if I had answered the question, everyone laughed and Vasconcellos replied in a friendly tone, "Yes indeed, that's enough!"

Chairman Vasconcellos "called for the question." I had been the only person to speak in favor of the resolution but no one had spoken against it. ACR 171 was unanimously approved by the committee.

Since bills must be approved by both the Assembly and Senate, Senator Petris of Alameda County sponsored the resolution in the Senate. It was adopted, it was recorded by the Secretary of State, and on September 10, 1976, ACR 171 became official.

However, with the passage of ACR 171, the university still refused to budge. Correspondence between the nonsigners and university officials continued through the last months of 1976 and the first months of 1977.

The pressure put upon the university by Assemblyman Knox was decisive. He had been as irritated as the nonsigners by the recalcitrance of the university. On March 16, 1977, he sent a letter to Glenn S. Dumke, then Chancellor of the California State University and Colleges, that expressed his feelings:

Last year I secured passage of ACR 171 which called attention to the California Supreme Court holding that an employee who was discharged solely for refusal to sign the Levering Oath, was entitled to reinstatement and requesting that the Trustees of the State University and Colleges reinstate any persons so discharged who desire reinstatement. It's been brought to my attention that Frank A. Rowe fits that category and has not been reinstated in the Art Department at San Francisco State University. Instead, his name has been entered in an "active" file. I ask you, now, why this sidestepping of the plain intent of the Supreme Court decision in the case of *Monroe* v. *Trustees*

of the California State Colleges, 6 Cal 3rd 399? How many others
have received this same kind of treatment?

I believe that Assemblyman Knox's letter convinced the
university administrators that they must stop stalling. Knox, one
of the most influential members of the legislature, was then
speaker *pro tempore* of the Assembly and a member of important
committees. Continued delay might hurt relationships with the
legislature, the administrators probably reasoned, which would
be a large price to pay just to block our reinstatement.

In any case, John Beecher received an offer of appointment,
just three days after the chancellor received Knox's letter, which
he accepted. My name came out of the "active" file, and it wasn't
long before I, too, was offered an appointment. Phiz Mezey
would finally be offered an appointment also, but not until two
semesters later. I made an appointment with the art department
chairman, believing that he would meet me with hostility.
Instead, he met us with great warmth when Marguerite and I
entered his office. We talked about classes that might fit my
backgound and parted amiably.

With a great feeling of emotion, I met John Beecher at his
office on the San Francisco State campus on the first day of the fall
semester—I had only about fifteen minutes before my first class
was to begin. Our conversation was as close as anyone came to a
ceremony celebrating our first day back at the school we had left
so abruptly twenty-seven years earlier. I had determined to return
unannounced. In fact, I only confided my part in the oath story to
one or two students at about the mid-semester date because I
didn't want that to influence anyone's judgment of my teaching.

My colleagues in the art department could not have been
more friendly and cooperative. Seymour Locks, my old friend
from the Beckmann class, the same gentle teacher who had first
brought me to State, reminisced with me about 1950. I was
particularly pleased when I was offered the same assignment for
another semester; the offer showed that I was not simply being
tolerated because of the legislature's actions. I turned down the
offer reluctantly because of my full teaching schedule at Laney
and chairmanship of that college's art department.

We had a party in the Life Drawing Studio on the last day
of the semester. Marguerite brought a salad, students brought
bread, cheeses, and cold cuts, and I supplied the beverages and
phonograph records. We talked about what we had accomplished
that semester. Then it was time to make a little speech. I told the
students that, in addition to whatever they might have picked up
about drawing, our class was something of a historic event,
a symbol of the end of a repressive loyalty oath.

I answered a few of their questions about the twenty-seven-
year period since my first experience at State. I emphasized that
what had been won was only a partial victory, since the state had
made no move to compensate us for our financial losses. Someone asked if I had learned anything from the long ordeal. I replied
that I had learned a number of things. One was the importance of
hanging on, of refusing to believe that all is lost. I had also learned
that the Bill of Rights is undoubtedly one of the great documents
of human history, but that when our civil rights are under fire, as
they were in the so-called McCarthy period, the rights of free
speech, press, and assembly are apt to be considered a hindrance.
An enemy among us, of far greater danger than the political
heretics they pretend to control, will always be the demagogues
waiting to play on the fears of the people.

I said that the socialist ideal expressed by the saying "From
each according to his ability; to each according to his needs," had
remained untarnished through all the trials and tribulations of
the decades that had just passed.

Another lesson, I said, was that schools in California aren't
organized in the sense of faculty, as the word was once defined,
that is, students and teachers learning and advancing their knowledge together *without political interference*. A layer cake might
be a fair analogy to the actual situation, with students on the
bottom (everyone laughed), teachers forming the middle layer,
and administrators next in a sort of gooey, faceless mass, and the
public and their political representatives a rich frosting on the
top of the cake.

"What's the point?" another student demanded. "Would
you prefer a nice pudding?" The point, I replied, was that the

132

Levering Loyalty Oath might never have existed were it not
for our layer-cake education system.

Another student asked, "Would you do it again?" I said
I hoped I would, and that in fact I had never done anything more
right than refusing to sign the unconstitutional Levering Oath.
We toasted that and then I turned in my students' grades to the
department secretary. Most were A's, a number were B's—
nothing lower.

Chapter 16

I N MY STATEMENT of October 1950, published in the college newspaper, I promised to protest "until the wrong done to the people of California by the Levering Loyalty Oath has been rectified." Our reinstatement was evidence that disclaimer oaths and witch-hunts had been discredited as political instruments. I felt that I had made a point.

But the fact remained that the nonsigners had suffered financial losses that the state refused to consider. John Beecher was in his seventies but had to go on working (he went to his classes in a wheelchair with an oxygen tank strapped to his back) because his long exile had prevented him from accumulating any retirement benefits. And, of course, the university-level teachers weren't the only ones who had suffered. How about reinstatement and compensation for people who had been social workers, bus drivers, hospital orderlies, and teachers in the elementary and high schools, and all the other public employees who had made a stand against the oath in 1950? With these thoughts in mind, I filed another claim with the State Board of Control in late 1977 (any further attempt to win redress through a court action would have been futile because the statutory limits had long since passed, no thanks to many of the attorneys I knew) and I wrote to all of the nonsigners I could locate, urging them to file claims. And I continued to urge our supporters in the legislature to introduce new legislation to extend the rights of reinstatement

and compensation to all areas of public service.

Again, Marguerite and I went back to Sacramento for my hearing. As we waited at the back of the hearing room, we tried to guess the identity of the State University lawyer. Marguerite thought he might be the slight, grey-haired man seated near us with a briefcase, working on his notes. She was right. The board chairman asked me to state my case and asked the university attorney to come forward. I was nervous, but Marguerite said later that my arguments were quite clear.

The attorney responded, prefacing his remarks with a comment that he was "wearing a black hat." His entire statement was on the one hand a tribute to the nonsigners, while on the other, a legal refutation of my claim. When the board voted to deny my claim, the chairman said he announced the decision with regret but that the legal position of the university was clear. The failure of ACR 171 to specifically mandate back pay was cited as the reason for the denial.

As we waited for the elevator, the university lawyer said he wanted to shake my hand. "Everyone should be grateful to you," he said. "The Constitution is stronger for your actions. You have won a moral victory!" I thanked him, thinking that I couldn't have been done in by a nicer guy.

But the rejection of my claim did not end the efforts to obtain compensation. Assemblyman Meldon E. Levine became interested in the story of the nonsigners, I believe through

articles he had read about John Beecher. Mr. Levine introduced
Assembly Bill 3026 in March 1978.[1] A portion of that proposal
reads as follows:

It is the Legislature's findings that one of the best ways to restore
the people's trust in government is that when the government acts
wrongfully, government takes action to right those wrongs.

This remark was followed by a provision for the appropriation of an unspecified amount of money to compensate the
San Francisco State nonsigners.

The bill got as far as the Assembly Ways and Means
Committee that spring. Marguerite and I attended the hearing.
The members of that committee agreed that the state had a moral
obligation to the nonsigners. But, they said, it would be impossible to appropriate more than a token amount in a year when
taxes were on the minds of everyone. Fifty thousand dollars for
each of the San Francisco State nonsigners was decided upon.

A big setback followed this decision in the form of
Proposition 13, the Jarvis-Gann tax measure, which was
approved by the voters just days after the Ways and Means
Committee met to decide on our compensation bill. The Jarvis-
Gann measure meant that essential services such as schools, fire
and police departments, and libraries would be hard pressed for
funds. In response to Proposition 13, the entire legislature voted
to eliminate any State program not already funded and costing
in excess of $100,000, effectively killing the compensation
proposal.

Assemblyman Levine assured us that he would revive
his proposal if the political climate improved. Moreover, he
conducted a correspondence with members of the State Board of
Control that resulted in a greater awareness among the board
members of their responsibilities to us. He urged us to file
claims. For me, this would be the third try.

Marguerite and I went to board meetings in June and in
August. The first, in Los Angeles, was postponed because one
member of the board was absent. The second, in Sacramento,
was also postponed to a date in October so I could rewrite my

claim. I had based my monetary loss upon the Vogel decision in 1967 while the board wanted all claims to be based upon a similar formula, out-of-pocket loss from 1950.

Then, in October 1979, the big hearing was held. In addition to myself, John Beecher, Phiz Mezey, Dr. Eason Monroe's widow, the widow of Glenn Carrico (Mrs. Wood), and Dr. Harry Steinmetz, the professor of psychology from San Diego, were all scheduled to speak.

The newspaper reported that the hearing was like a time warp, with those grey and wrinkled men and women talking about something that had happened in 1950. Each of the six claimants made a statement. A representative of the State University and Colleges said, "It is unfortunate that we have not dealt with men of principle as fairly as we might at all times." At last, the California State University and Colleges trustees were supporting our claim.

The State Board of Control voted to recommend to the legislature that a token $25,000 award be made to each of the six claimants. The amount represented only 15 percent of the amount the claimants determined to be their real loss. The *Sacramento Bee* reported that everyone groaned when they heard the amount announced. I felt a little bit ashamed. We were beginning to forget what the Levering Oath fight had been about.

In January 1980, the State Senate held a hearing to decide if the state should set aside the money needed to implement the recommendation of the Board of Control. Only a few days before, on December 17, 1979, Soviet troops had occupied Afghanistan. In Iran, 50 American hostages were being held by a mob incited by a shaky government. The entire Middle East might fall to the Communists. Marguerite and I read that bomb shelter sales had increased by one-third since the Soviet incursion in Afghanistan. An anonymous caller who said he was a member of a group called the Patriotic Scuba Divers telephoned a radio station to say that he had placed a mine in the Sacramento River to block the sailing of a Soviet grain ship, causing the closing of the shipping channel. Marguerite and I could feel the hysteria rising again. The enemy among us was there—in the Senate hearing room.

A few questions were asked of the representative of the Board of Control, who presented our claim. One senator suggested that we should have gone to teach somewhere other than California if we had not wanted to sign the Levering Oath in 1950. Over the objections of Assemblyman Levine, they voted the compensation recommendation down, unanimously. At the time of this writing, there is no way to know if anything more will come of this matter.

Not everyone that saith unto me, Lord, Lord, shall enter into the kingdom of heaven, but he that doeth the will of my Father . . . .

Matthew 7:21

ACKNOWLEDGEMENTS

CONSIDERABLE RESEARCH WAS DONE to ascertain the accuracy of facts stated in this book. The assistance of Marguerite, my wife and comrade for over thirty years, was invaluable in recalling details and in proofreading. Our daughters also contributed, Nancy with her paper, *The Loyalty Oath*, written as a college research project, and Georgia, who offered constructive criticism.

Assemblyman John Vasconcellos and Assemblyman John Knox put together the legislation that brought the story closer to a just ending. Assemblyman Meldon Levine and his staff, Annette Porini, Robyn Boyer, Laura Kaplan, and Catherine Unger, have my undying thanks for their efforts on behalf of the nonsigners.

The support of Jackie Wynne and Gary Deurner, both on the staff of the California State University and Colleges, is much appreciated.

The United Professors of California and the Peralta Federation of Teachers, Local 1603 (and particularly Leroy Voto and Jenette Golds) have been generous with their support.

I want to thank my friends in the Mills College community for helping me to return to school in middle age, and to remember the late Tony Prieto, the chairman of the Mills College Art Department at that time, for his encouragement.

Amelia Fry, of the Regional Oral History Program, Bancroft Library, Berkeley; Mary McWilliam, of the J. Paul Leonard Library, California State University, San Francisco; the staff of the Meiklejohn Civil Liberties Institute, Berkeley; and the staffs of the Oakland Library and the Contra Costa County Central Library were all very generous with their time and assistance.

Edward R. Long, a doctoral candidate in history at the University of California, San Diego, has been helpful in checking facts. If an error in detail or date still exists, it is in an area where he could not possibly have had knowledge. Clayton Barbeau read my manuscript in an early stage and helped to put things in proper order. Michael Furay of Laney College made valuable suggestions.

Judge Paul Halvonik, as counsel for the ACLU in 1971, was generous with advice and supportive documents. Dorothy Ehrlich of the American Civil Liberties Union and Karl Feichtmeir, Manuscript Curator, California Historical Society, assisted in making documents available.

I appreciate the consideration of State Board of Control members David Janssen, Peter Pelkofer, and Edwin Beach. Staff members Fred Duenrostro and Gary Longholm were especially kind.

NOTES

Chapter 1

[1]Leonard Rapport and Arthur Northwood, Jr., *Rendevous With Destiny: A History of the 101st Airborne Division,* Infantry Journal Press, 1948.

[2]Representative John S. Wood, then chairman of the House Committee on Un-American Activities.

[3]Harold M. Hyman, *To Try Men's Souls,* University of California Press, 1959.

[4]References to the Reinecke case in Hawaii and the Los Angeles loyalty program are based upon copies of court records on file at the Meiklejohn Civil Liberties Institute, Berkeley, California.

[5]Background incidents illustrating the repression of 1947–49 can be found in many newspapers of that period.

[6]Carey McWilliams, *Witch Hunt: The Revival of Heresy,* Little, Brown, 1950.

[7]The Canwell Committee hearings at the University of Washington are described in Melvin Rader, *False Witness,* University of Washington Press, 1969.

Chapter 2

[1]David P. Gardner, *The California Oath Controversy,* University of California Press, 1967; and George R. Stewart, *The Year of the Oath: The Fight for Academic Freedom at the University of California,* Doubleday, 1950.

[2]Edward R. Long, Ph.D. dissertation in history, University of California, San Diego, 1980.

[2]Alexander Meiklejohn, *Political Freedom: The Constitutional Powers of the People,* Harper and Bros., 1948.

Chapter 3

[1]Many of the incidents in this book are based upon stories that appeared in the *Golden Gater,* San Francisco State College.

[2]Governor Warren's remarks to the Disabled American Veterans Convention were reported in the San Francisco *Chronicle* on August 16, 1950.

³The Levering Oath was appended to the traditional Oath of Allegiance. Both are reprinted in this book following the preface for purposes of comparison. The entire Levering Act appears as an appendix to this memoir. The reader should read it in full to understand the civil defense provisions of the law.

⁴See "The Political Context of McCarthyism," *The Review of Politics,* January 1971, for reference to the McCarran Act.

Chapter 4

¹The Reverend Harry C. Meserve was Minister of the First Unitarian Church at Franklin and Geary Streets, San Francisco. In October 1950, he delivered a Sunday sermon entitled "What is Loyalty?" Printed copies of this sermon were distributed at the Sunday service.

²*The Golden Gater,* San Francisco State College.

³Editors and leaders of the Student Committee for Academic Freedom are listed in the *SCAF Newsletter,* No. 2, October 23, 1950.

⁴Members of the "Committee of Ten" were professors Monroe (chairman), Beecher, Bisno, F. Cave, R. Cave, McKenna, Outland, Pockman, Schneider, and Treutlein.

⁵The complete statement of the American Association of University Professors, San Francisco State College, appears as an appendix to this memoir.

Chapter 5

¹In my opinion, the most scholarly study of the events of 1950, as they developed in the legislature, is Edward R. Long, *Earl Warren and the Politics of Anti-Communism* (in manuscript). Mr. Long's book will be published in the near future. He has generously shared his notes for that comprehensive work.

²Sources for material on this exchange were California *Journal of the Senate,* 1950 Third Extraordinary Session, pp. 85–87; *San Francisco Chronicle,* September 25, 1950; *San Francisco Examiner,* September 25, 1950; *People's World,* September 27, 1950.

Chapter 6

¹My references to the psychology of oaths are based primarily on my memory of the event, but have been reinforced by the following: Nancy Rowe, *The Loyalty Oath,* 1971 (unpublished research paper); and Morton Grodzins, *The Loyal and the Disloyal,* University of Chicago Press, 1956.

Chapter 7

¹Seventeen lines from John Beecher, "The Search for Truth," *Collected Poems 1924– 1974,* Macmillan © 1956, 1960, 1974. In a letter dated February 24, 1975, and in response to my letter informing him that I was trying to put together a memoir about the Levering Oath, John Beecher wrote the following: "I received your monograph concurrently with a letter from Nancy McDermid. I read your painstaking and able account through at a sitting. I will of course go over it again and send you detailed comments as well as any suggestions I may have for improving it. I fail to understand your lack of faith in it. Such comments as 'Burn it if you want to' are absolutely shocking. I am particularly touched by your generosity to myself in the account, and the apt quotations from my poems. This acknowledgment by you compensates to a real degree for all the neglect and put-downs over the 25 years since 1950. I really thank you for this."

[2]Claude Bourdet, *The Nation,* December 12, 1953. This quote by Bourdet was also used in the book that I would recommend to every history teacher interested in conveying the essence of life in the United States from the 1920s to the 1980s, *The Education of Carey McWilliams,* Simon & Schuster, 1978.

[3]All quotes and references to Phiz Mezey can be documented in the *SCAF Newsletter,* No. 2, October 23, 1950; and the *Golden Gater,* October 26, 1950.

[4]The debate between Professor Bisno and Mr. Van Pinney was reported in Federation for Repeal of the Levering Act, *REPEAL Newsletter,* December 1950.

Chapter 8

[1]Dr. Monroe's statements were reported in *Fear is Like a Cancer,* a publication of the Federation for Repeal of the Levering Act.

[2]Reports of the incidents described in this chapter can be found in November 1950 issues of the San Francisco *Chronicle;* the San Francisco *Examiner;* and the *Oakland Tribune.*

[3]Edwin Broun Fred was quoted in a publication of San Francisco's First Unitarian Church, in October 1950.

Chapter 9

[1]All references to Dr. J. Paul Leonard can be found in quotations and biographical data taken from the San Francisco *Chronicle,* February 5, 1953; and the *Contra Costa Times,* June 5, 1977.

[2]Joseph Alioto's remarks were also reported in the February 5, 1953, San Francisco *Chronicle.*

[3]An excellent picture of the November 13, 1950, farewell rally sponsored by the Student Committee for Academic freedom (SCAF) was published in the *Oakland Tribune* on September 20, 1977, in an article intended to memorialize the oath struggle.

[4]Robert M. Hutchins' remarks were reported in David Caute, *The Great Fear: The Anti-Communist Purge under Truman and Eisenhower, Simon & Schuster, 1978.*

Chapter 10

[1]*Witch Hunt: The Revival of Heresy,* Little, Brown, 1950. McWilliams' remarks in *The Education of Carey McWilliams* are an interesting aside on the political climate of 1950: "Once again my timing was or seemed to be impeccable. I had written a book about McCarthyism which was completed so soon after McCarthy's famous Wheeling, West Virginia, speech of February 9, 1950, in which he made his national debut as an 'anti-Communist' demagogue, that I could refer to it only in the introduction. By the time copies arrived in California in early November, the witch-hunt was well under way, but apparently few people wanted to read about it just then. Perhaps they were too preoccupied with the subject, or they may have been merely inattentive. Whatever the reason, the sales were not impressive; the book sells better today, in a reprint edition, than it did then."

[2]Eddie Tangen is referred to in Caute, *The Great Fear.*

[3]My recollection of the American Civil Liberties Union policies in the 1940s and 1950s (no longer in effect, so far as I know), and the withdrawal of support from John Beecher and myself, can be confirmed in the *Board Minutes* for October and November, 1950; American Civil Liberties Union, Northern California. The *Board Minutes* are filed with the California Historical Society in San Francisco. Other studies of ACLU policies are

Markmann's book, cited in the text (St. Martin's Press, 1965) and Corliss Lamont (Ed.), *The Trial of Elizabeth Gurley Flynn by the American Civil Liberties Union*, Modern Reader Paperbacks, 1968.

[1]In a letter to the author dated January 25, 1980, Mr. Ernest Besig wrote, "Under the leadership of the Rt. Rev. Edward L. Parsons, Dr. Alexander Meiklejohn, Helen Salz and others, the Northern California branch strenuously opposed the resolution and its progeny and as the local executive director I argued for its repeal at biennial conferences." In the same letter, Besig stated, "under Board policy, we also insisted upon sole representation and refused to participate in joint defenses or united fronts."

[2]According to the ACLU Northern California branch *Board Minutes*, on file at the California Historical Society in San Francisco, the board members attending the meeting of November 2, 1950, were as follows: Bishop Parsons presiding; present Mssrs. Besig, Adams, Brill, Caldwell, Campo, Green, Kennedy, Manning and Meiklejohn; Margaret Hayes, Ruth Kingman, Helen Salz, and Kathleen D. Tolman.

Chapter 11

[1]The action of the Third District Court of Appeal with reference to the University of California Regents' Oath appeared in the San Francisco *Chronicle* on April 7, 1951.

[2]San Francisco *Chronicle* on May 23, 1951. Richard E. Combs, chief counsel for the state Un-American Activities Committee stated at that time, "The teaching profession is a particularly suspect group because of its contact with impressionable youth. The teachers have a higher duty than to defend the tender carcass of academic freedom."

Hursel W. Alexander, representing the Communist Party of California, also applied for lobbying credentials on May 22, 1951. He was turned down because membership in the Communist Party was evidence of lack of "good moral character."

[3]Quotations by Mrs. Carrico and her sons are taken from letters to the author.

[4]In connection with my remarks on abstract expressionism, it is interesting to note that Clement Greenberg, a leading theorist of avant-garde art in the 1950s, was threatened with a libel suit for his baiting of the distinguished editor, J. Alvarez del Vayo, of *The Nation*. This incident can be confirmed by reading *The New Leader* for May 19, 1951.

[5]San Francisco *Chronicle*, October 12, 1979.

[6]The constitutional amendment hearing was reported in the San Francisco *Chronicle* on March 21, 1951, under the headline: "Two Protestors Ejected—Assembly Unit Approves Loyalty Plan."

[7]Judge Ransome Longacre's remark appeared in a 1962 edition of the *Oakland Tribune*.

Chapter 12

[1]John Beecher's life as a rancher is described in his poem, "Reflections of a Man Who Once Stood Up for Freedom," *Collected Poems, 1924–1974*, Macmillan, ©1956, 1960, 1974.

[2]My feelings about Eisenhower were mixed. I had admired him during the war and had even spoken to him once when he reviewed the 101st Airborne Division at Mourmelon Le Grande, France. As he came up to me, Eisenhower asked, "How's the food in your outfit?" "Just fine, sir," I replied, even though it was lousy. (So much for my acquaintance with the Commander of the Allied Expeditionary Forces.) When I followed his later career, I was embarrassed for him, thinking that he should have quit when he was ahead. But Eisenhower's speech on the military-industrial complex was a real redeemer.

[3]Reported in William Lawrence, *Six Presidents,* Saturday Review Press, 1972. Milton S. Eisenhower, the president's brother, says it never happened.

[4]Senator Porter's remarks are in the *Congressional Record.*

[5]Dr. Holland Roberts had taught at Stanford University prior to his work with the California Labor School.

[6]Communist Party statistics are from Caute, *The Great Fear.*

Chapter 13

[1]All the facts concerning the hearing by the House Committee on Un-American Activities are in the San Francisco *Chronicle* for June 18, 19, and 20, 1957.

[2]Tom Hardwick has a tape recording of the entire hearing of June 18, 1957.

[3]Mrs. Barbara Sherwood filed suit against the government for the wrongful death of her husband. I contacted Mr. Bertram Edises, who was her attorney. He informed me that Mrs. Sherwood's suit was not successful.

[4]From *Collected Poems, 1924–1974,* Macmillan © 1956, 1960, 1974. Seventeen lines from ''The Search for Truth'' and the entire poem ''Inquest.''

[5]Barbara Garson's statement appeared in a leaflet sponsored by the End-the-Oath Defense Fund, 2411 Grove Street, Berkeley, California, and was endorsed by American Federation of Teachers, Local 1570.

[6]San Francisco *Chronicle,* January 24, 1967.

[7]San Francisco *Chronicle,* January 12, 1967.

[8]In the Superior Court of the State of California for the County of Los Angeles; *Robert S. Vogel,* Plaintiff, v. *County of Los Angeles,* Defendant. No. 907,984; May 25, 1967.

[9]San Francisco *Chronicle,* August 17, 1967.

Chapter 14

[1]Dr. Summerskill wrote on June 6, 1968, ''As you must know, I am the last person in California who could assist you at this time.''

[2]January 9, 1968.

[3]August 1, 1968.

[4]September 12, 1968.

[5]April 13, 1971.

[6]In the Supreme Court of the State of California, In Bank; *Albert E. Monroe,* Plaintiff and Appellant v. *Trustees of the California State Colleges,* Defendant and Respondent; LA 29926 Super. Ct., 944-675, filed December 30, 1967.

[7]The *Inner City Mother Goose* story refers to *Clark Natwick* v. *State Board of Education,* reported in an AFT Teacher Rights *Newsletter.*

Chapter 15

[1]See the appendix for the text of ACR 171.

[2]Copies of correspondence between Assemblyman Knox and the trustees are in the possession of the author.

Chapter 16

[1]See the appendix for the text of AB 3026.

APPENDICES

A. Full text of the Levering Oath
B. A Declaration of Disapproval of the Levering Oath by the Membership of the San Francisco State College Chapter of the American Association of University Professors
C. Assembly Concurrent Resolution No. 171
D. Assembly Bill No. 3026

A. Full Text of the Levering Act

3100. It is hereby declared that the defense of the civil population during the present state of world affairs is of paramount state importance requiring the undivided attention and best efforts of our citizens. In furtherance of such defense and in the exercise of police power of the State in protection of its citizens, all public employees are hereby declared to be civil defense workers subject to such civilian defense activities as may be assigned to them by their superiors or by law.

3101. For the purpose of the chapter the term "civil defense worker" includes all public employees and all volunteers in any civilian defense organization accredited by the State Disaster council. The term "public employees" includes all persons employed by the State or any county, city, city and county, state agency or public district, excluding aliens legally employed.

3102. Subject to the provisions of Section 3 of Article XX of the Constitution, all civil defense workers shall within the first 30 days of employment take and subscribe to the oath or affirmation required by this chapter.

3103. The oath or affirmation required by this chapter is as follows: "I, _____, do solemnly swear (or affirm) that I will support and defend the Constitution of the United States and Constitution of the State of California against all enemies, foreign and domestic; that I will bear true faith and allegiance to the Constitution of the United States and the Constitution of the State of California; that I take this obligation freely, without any mental reservation or purpose of evasion; and that I will well and faithfully discharge the duties upon which I am about to enter. And I do further swear (or affirm) that I do not advocate, nor am I a member of any party or organization, political or otherwise, that now advocates the overthrow of the Government of the United States or of the State of California by force or violence or other unlawful means; that within the five years immediately preceding the taking of this oath (or affirmation) I have not been a member of any party or organization, political or otherwise, that advocated the overthrow of the Government of the United States or of the

State of California by force or violence or other unlawful means except as follows: _____ (If no affiliations, write in the words "No Exceptions") and that during such time as I am a member or employee of the _____ (Name of public agency) I will not advocate nor become a member of any party or organization, political or otherwise, that advocates the overthrow of the Government of the United States or of the State of California by force or violence or other unlawful means.

3104. The oath or affirmation may be taken before any officer authorized to administer oaths.

3105. The oath or affirmation of any civil defense worker of the State shall be filed with the State Personnel Board within 30 days of the date on which it is taken and subscribed. The oath or affirmation of any civil defense worker of any county shall be filed in the office of the county clerk of the county. The oath or affirmation of any civil defense worker of any city shall be filed in the office of the city clerk of the city. The oath or affirmation of any civil defense worker of any other agency or district, shall be filed with such officer or employee of the agency or district as may be designated by such agency or district.

3106. Compliance with this chapter shall, as to state employees, be deemed full compliance with Chapter 4, Part 1, Division 5, Title 2 of this code, requiring taking of oaths by state employees.

3107. No compensation nor reimbursement for expenses incurred shall be paid to any civil defense worker by any public agency unless such civil defense worker has taken and subscribed to the oath or affirmation required by this chapter. It shall be the duty of the person certifying to public payrolls to ascertain and certify that such civil defense worker has taken such oath and affirmation.

3108. Every person who, while taking and subscribing to the oath or affirmation required by this chapter, states as true any material which he knows to be false, is guilty of perjury, and is punishable by imprisonment in the state prison not less than one nor more than 14 years.

3109. Every person having taken and subscribed to the oath or affirmation required by this chapter, who, while in the employ of, or service with, the State or any county, city, city and county, state agency, public district, or civilian defense organization advocates or becomes a member of any party or organization, political or otherwise, that advocates the overthrow of the Government of the United States by force or violence or other unlawful means, is guilty of a felony, and is punishable by imprisonment in the state prison not less than one nor more than 14 years.

Sec. 2. Subject to the provisions of Section 3 of Article XX of the Constitution, all persons designated in Chapter 8, Division 4, Title 1, of the Government Code as civil defense workers, on the effective date of this act shall, within 30 days, take and subscribe to the oath or affirmation required by Chapter 8, Division 4, Title 1, of the Government Code. Any public employee who is on authorized leave on the thirtieth day after the effective date of this act shall take and subscribe said oath or affirmation within 30 days of his return to work.

Sec. 3. If any provision of this act or the application thereof to any person or circumstances is held invalid, such invalidity shall not affect other provisions or applications of the act which can be given effect without the invalid provision or application, and to this end the provisions of this act are declared to be severable.

Sec. 4. This act is an urgency measure necessary for the immediate preservation of the public peace, health or safety within the meaning of Article IV of the Constitution and shall go into immediate effect. The facts constituting such necessity are: During the present emergency in world affairs loyalty and allegiance to the United States and the principles for which it stands are of utmost importance. Immediate assurance that persons in civil defense are loyal to this government and are not in fact advocates of its overthrow by force and violence is essential to the well-being of the State and Nation and the confidence of the people. It is therefore necessary that this act take effect immediately.

B. A Declaration of Disapproval of the Levering Oath by the Membership of the San Francisco State College Chapter of the American Association of University Professors

We believe that the act is unnecessary. As employees of the State of California, we have already signed a positive and comprehensive oath of loyalty. We submit the record of our years of faithful and patriotic service to the State and the Nation as genuine evidence of our loyalty.

We believe that the act is a product of political hysteria. The legislature took only five days to pass this bill which so vitally affects at least a million citizens in our State. Twelve days after its introduction, the law was signed by the Governor. Surely, careful and thoughtful deliberation did not attend the enactment of this law.

We believe that the act is ambiguous. We are asked to sign a document which no one can accurately interpret. Under these circumstances, common sense dictates caution and concern. We can sign this oath only with fear and uncertainty.

We believe that the act violates the State Constitution. Article 20, Section 3, of the State Constitution specifically states: "No other oath, declaration, or test shall be required as a qualification for any office or public trust."

We believe that the act sets up a political test for employment. The requirement of this oath is an act of political discrimination, prohibiting, on penalty of dismissal, any public employee from membership in a legal political party of his choice. We deplore and oppose this assignment of public servants to the status of second-class citizenship.

We believe that the act undermines tenure and professional security. Previously, employees on permanent tenure could be dismissed only on grounds of incompetence or immorality. They may now be separated from public employ if, in following the dictates of their consciences, they cannot comply with this law.

We believe that the act weakens the bargaining rights of public employees. In the face of rising costs of living and increasing taxation, this law has the effect, through intimidation, if not through specific provisions, of discouraging organized effort of any group of public employees to seek fair adjustment of salaries and working conditions.

We believe that the act is an attack on civil liberty. Advanced as a safeguard to democracy, this law actually threatens democracy. Freedom of speech is a cornerstone of democracy. This freedom implies and guarantees freedom of belief. To be free to believe and to speak — hence, to advocate — is a basic right of every American citizen. To advocate a belief and to act criminally against the people of the State or Nation are clearly and objectively distinguishable. Criminal code is the appropriate instrument for the apprehension and punishment of the criminal.

We believe that the act is an attack upon academic freedom. Good teaching is based upon the teacher's freedom to think, to investigate, to believe, to doubt, to criticize, and otherwise to pursue the truth with clear and honest conscience. Without this freedom there can be no teaching . . . only propagandizing. The control of thought is the familiar device of those who have sought to overwhelm democracy by repressive legislation and military might. To control the thought of either the citizen or the teacher is to destroy his thinking.

We believe that the act may be a forerunner of further threats and repressions. We fear that this law is but the first step in further repressive measures to deny us and others the rights and privileges of democratic citizens and teachers.

We believe that this act opens the floodgate of smear attacks and intimidation. Trial by irresponsible accusations, attacks by disgruntled persons, and guilt by association are among the host of personal and professional injuries set loose upon us by this law. Special interest groups, for their own selfish purposes, may find this act a ready weapon to use against individuals or groups in public employ.

October 1950

C. Assembly Concurrent Resolution No. 171

Introduced by Assemblymen Vasconcellos and Knox

March 15, 1976
Referred to Committee on Education

Assembly Concurrent Resolution No. 171—Relative to higher education.

Legislative Counsel's Digest

ACR 171, as introduced, Vasconcellos (Ed.). Public higher education.

Requests Trustees of California State University and Colleges to report to the Legislature the names of all persons discharged for refusing to sign the so-called "Levering" loyalty oath, their current employment situation, and whether they desire to be reinstated. It also requests the trustees to reinstate persons so desiring.

Fiscal committee: no.

WHEREAS, During the 1950's and 1960's many public employees, particularly in the field of education, were discharged or denied employment solely for conscientiously refusing to sign the so-called Levering oath contained in Section 3 of Article XX of the State Constitution; and

WHEREAS, In the 1967 case of *Vogel* v. *County of Los Angeles,* 68 Cal. 2d 18, the California Supreme Court held the Levering oath to be invalid as an unconstitutional violation of the first amendment of the Constitution of the United States, making such discharge or denial of employment unjustifiable and wrong; and

WHEREAS, In the 1971 case of *Monroe* v. *Trustees of the California State Colleges,* 6 Cal. 3d 399, the California Supreme Court held that an employee who was discharged by the Trustees of the California State Colleges solely for refusal to sign the Levering oath was entitled to reinstatement; and

WHEREAS, In the years since the Monroe case, there has been little if any reinstatement by the Trustees of the California State University and Colleges of persons wrongfully discharged for refusal to take the Levering oath; now, therefore, be it

Resolved by the Assembly of the State of California, the Senate thereof concurring, That the Trustees of the California State University and Colleges are requested to report to the Legislature the names of all persons so discharged and their current employment situation, and whether they desire to be reinstated; and be it further

Resolved, That the trustees are requested to reinstate any persons so discharged, and who desire reinstatement; and be it further

Resolved, That a copy of this resolution be transmitted to the Trustees of the California State University and Colleges.

D. Assembly Bill No. 3026

Introduced by Assemblyman Levine

March 21, 1978
Referred to Committee on Education

An act relating to higher education, and making an appropriation therefore.

Legislative Counsel's Digest

AB 3026, as introduced, Levine (Ed.). CSUC: former employees wrongfully discharged.

From 1950 through 1954, 10 employees of the then California State Colleges were discharged solely for refusing to sign the so-called Levering loyalty oath which subsequently was held to be unconstitutional by the California Supreme Court.

This bill would appropriate an unspecified amount from the General Fund to the Department of Finance for awarding lost pay and pension benefits to the above specified employees, as computed in a particular manner. If the employee has died, his or her living spouse or living issue or issues would receive the award in a specified manner.

Vote: ⅔. Appropriation: yes. Fiscal committee: yes. State-mandated local program: no.

The people of the State of California do enact as follows:

SECTION 1. The Legislature finds that in the post-World War II period, 10 employees of the then California State Colleges were discharged solely for conscientiously refusing to sign the so-called Levering loyalty oath contained in Section 3 of Article XX of the California Constitution. The Legislature further finds that the California Supreme Court subsequently held such oath to be invalid as an unconstitutional restriction on the freedom of association as protected by the First Amendment to the United States Constitution and held, in one instance, that an employee so

155

discharged would be entitled to lost pay and pension benefits that accrued after his right to reinstate arose. Furthermore, the legislature finds that at the direction of the Legislature, the Trustees of the California State University and Colleges have offered to reinstate all former employees who were discharged solely for refusing to sign the so-called Levering loyalty oath.

It is the Legislature's finding that it is reasonable to believe that one of the best ways to restore the people's trust in government is that when the government acts wrongfully, government takes action to right those wrongs. Therefore, the Legislature declares that there is no violation of Section 6 of Article XVI of the California Constitution in enacting this act since the provisions of this act serve the public purpose of helping to restore the people's trust in government.

SEC. 2. There is hereby appropriated from the General Fund the sum of _____ dollars ($_____) to the Department of Finance for awarding lost pay and pension benefits to employees of the then California State Colleges who were discharged from 1950 through 1954 solely for refusing to sign the so-called Levering loyalty oath contained in Section 3 of Article XX of the California Constitution. In the event the employee has died, his or her lost pay and pension benefits shall be awarded to the employee's spouse who the employee was legally married to at the time of the employee's death or, if the deceased employee never had such a spouse or if any such spouse of the employee is also deceased, then to the employee's living issue or issues, if any, in equal shares. If the deceased employee has no such living spouse, issue, or issues, no award shall be made.

The amount of any award required to be made pursuant to this section shall be reduced by the amount of any previous awards made for lost pay and pension benefits, if any, and the amount of any award made pursuant to this section shall be the difference between the salary and pension benefits the employee would have earned if the employee had not been dismissed and the salary and pension benefits the employee earned in other employment. If the employee is alive upon the date this act becomes effective, salary and pension benefits shall be measured from the date he or she was discharged to the effective date of this act or the date the employee was reinstated by the California State University and Colleges, whichever came first. If the employee is deceased upon the date this act becomes effective, salary and pension benefits shall be measured from the date he or she was discharged to the date the employee died.

The Trustees of the California State University and Colleges shall assist the Department of Finance fully in making awards pursuant to this section.

157